If we could meet the Jesus in this [illegible]
would want to follow him.
James Catford, Chief Executive, Bible Society

Introductory courses like Alpha are effective invitations to Christian faith. As a consequence, many people feel the need for help in moving beyond the **invitation** to the work of **incorporation** into the Easter mystery in which we share in God's way of dying and living. What is special about John Valentine's book is that it sounds the depths of personal discipleship by relating our own lives to God's purposes of corporate and cosmic renewal. He writes with the hard-won clarity of someone who has known both pain and joy in a very fruitful ministry in central London among the diverse community which he serves.
Dr Richard Chartres, Bishop of London

This is a refreshingly realistic and inspiring book about what it means to be truly alive, and truly ourselves through following Jesus. For many Christians, how they live out their faith is full of uncertainties, limitations and unfulfilled expectations. Where many writers have glossed over this reality, John has faced it full on. Too often Christians have no vision, or a narrow vision, of what God wants to do in and through their lives. John casts a vision of what our lives could look like if we let God impact our work time as much as our home life and church involvement. He then helps us to think through how to apply this in the chaos and busyness of our day-to-day lives.

I would strongly encourage you to read this book, as I am convinced it will help many people to live a more vibrant and real life that leaves a deep impression on others.
Richard Gough, Finance and Trading Director of Tearfund

Critics of the Christian faith suggest it is restrictive, dehumanizing and oppressive. *Follow Me* demonstrates in practical and realistic ways how Christian discipleship makes us more fully human, not less so, calling us to live the whole of life as God intended. It is an ideal introduction

to Christian living, modelled on Jesus himself, rooted firmly in God's purposes of restoration in Christ, whilst directly addressing today's concerns for authenticity, identity, integrity and community.
Jonathan Lamb, Director of Langham Preaching, Langham Partnership International; Chairman, Keswick Ministries

There is a great deal of good, pure, distilled wisdom in this book. John Valentine writes with style, experience and a sure sense of what really matters in the Christian life.
The Revd Dr Graham Tomlin, Dean, St Mellitus College, London

'follow me'

John Valentine

'follow me'

becoming a liberated disciple

ivp

INTER-VARSITY PRESS
Norton Street, Nottingham NG7 3HR, England
Email: ivp@ivpbooks.com
Website: www.ivpbooks.com

First published 2009

British Library Cataloguing in Publication Data
A catalogue record for this book is available from the British Library.

ISBN 978–1–84474–394–0

Typeset by CRB Associates, Potterhanworth, Lincolnshire
Printed and bound in Great Britain by Ashford Colour Press Ltd, Gosport,
Hampshire

*Inter-Varsity Press publishes Christian books that are true to the Bible and that
communicate the gospel, develop discipleship and strengthen the church for its mission
in the world.*

*Inter-Varsity Press is closely linked with the Universities and Colleges Christian
Fellowship, a student movement connecting Christian Unions in universities and colleges
throughout Great Britain, and a member movement of the International Fellowship of
Evangelical Students. Website: www.uccf.org.uk*

Contents

Foreword

I have known John and Catherine Valentine for many years since John and I worked together as curates under Sandy Millar. They are a wonderful couple – full of Christian faith, wisdom and fun.

In his time at Holy Trinity, John was instrumental in building up the church's School of Theology – a job he did with enthusiasm and commitment and for which he was admirably qualified with his gift for academic scholarship. He is a skilled and popular preacher.

John and Catherine left Holy Trinity to lead a church plant at St George's Holborn, and from there they have built up a significant ministry in London. John's many gifts for explaining the Christian faith combine with a profound love for every individual, particularly those going through difficult times. His wisdom, humility and common sense as expressed in this book come from a strong Christian faith, which has grown stronger through the depths of personal experience and struggles.

Rev. Nicky Gumbel, vicar of Holy Trinity Brompton

Acknowledgments and dedication

I am very grateful to all those who have helped me so much to follow Jesus Christ in some small way. I want especially to thank my dear parents who first brought me to baptism and to church, and have shown me consistently what it is to live Christian lives.

I am hugely grateful too to James Catford and Simon Vernon. We meet up monthly to eat high-cholesterol breakfasts around London and to help one another copy Jesus in our lives. They have provided me with much wisdom, encouragement and laughter.

Many thanks to Eleanor Trotter at IVP for being such a kind and encouraging editor.

Most of all, I want to thank my darling wife Catherine who, although she denies it, is far ahead of me in following Jesus, and is the most holy and inspirational person I know. To her I gratefully dedicate this book.

Preface

'Christ did not die to make us Christians. He died to make us human.' So said Archbishop Oscar Romero who was shot dead, martyred for following Jesus in the face of government opposition.[1]

The great discovery for me in recent years is that following Jesus makes us more human, not less so. Even though he says things like 'whoever loses his life for me and for the gospel will save it',[2] he does so in the context of how we most truly discover ourselves. Jesus invites us to live life well, really well, far beyond contemporary society's bland definitions and assumptions about the good life. He gives us both virtue and exhilaration together – usually regarded as mutually incompatible. He offers us deep feeling and clear thinking. He invites us to a quality of life that is stronger than the grave itself. He sees things very differently from most of us, and much of his teaching is acutely uncomfortable. But, he insists, this is the path, the only path, to life that is really life – the life of God.

This book is neither a manual of church practice nor an exposition of the Christian faith. It is an invitation to follow Jesus, to trust him enough to pattern our very lives on his life. It is a call to give him everything, because, he says, that is the only way to discover ourselves.

The book has been percolating away for four years now, and much has happened in the writing of it. I wrote it first as a booklet for the church where I am privileged to be the Rector – St George's, Holborn, in the centre of London. When IVP kindly asked me to adapt it for a wider audience, I was delighted to do so. There then followed two immensely difficult and painful years. Friendships with dear friends were tragically lost. The church went through a firestorm. I myself became ill, and was signed off work with depression and anxiety. I thought I was losing everything. It was a dark period, but I am coming out of it. And I feel more strongly than ever that the teaching of Jesus, which I have tried to highlight here, is not something that belongs in a religious sub-culture, but a message for the world. It works – in the fires, as well as in the sunshine. This is life – not just superficial recipes for self-actualization or calm, but a real, profound, invitation to true life, to God-life.

The book is structured around a progression: from the personal to the corporate to the cosmic. It starts by looking at what it means for us as individuals to be called to follow Jesus Christ, and then relates that to how life in the church might fit in, before examining our role in God's plans for the whole of his world. This progression is born of the conviction that to follow Jesus is to follow him right into the heart of what God intends for the whole universe. A true following of Jesus can never be left at the purely personal level; it must involve God's plans for the renewal of all of humanity, and through this renewed human race nothing less than the liberation and transformation of the whole created order.

But the personal–corporate–cosmic progression is also born of the conviction that the potential for global impact is present from the very beginning for each of us as individuals when we follow Christ. It is our spiritual DNA. Growth as disciples will necessarily involve growth into the church, and from there into the world, unless growth becomes stunted or twisted.

The structure of the book can be pictured like this:

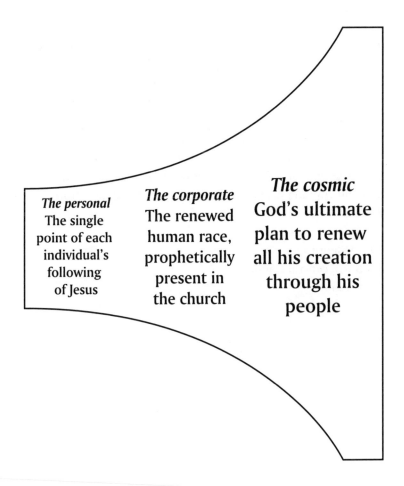

The personal
The single point of each individual's following of Jesus

The corporate
The renewed human race, prophetically present in the church

The cosmic
God's ultimate plan to renew all his creation through his people

Each aspect of following Jesus is integral to the next stage and grows out of it. But each aspect is also fully present as potential in each preceding stage. From the beginning we need the two parallel convictions: to follow Jesus is to enlist in something that has consequences for the whole universe and the whole human race; and, at the same time, this huge picture can only make sense, and can only be entered into, through our own lives being changed individually, and as we, one at a time, get involved in God's church.

This is where the focus lies of what it is to be a *liberated* disciple. It does not mean that we will necessarily be happy and fulfilled, or that all our dreams and aspirations will come to pass. But it does mean that we will be liberated from all our lesser concerns as we find the source, joy and meaning of our lives in God and his cosmic plans in Jesus Christ.

Dante's inferno had 'Abandon hope all you who enter here!' inscribed over the gates of hell. I therefore should like this book to say the opposite. This adventure of following Jesus, of trusting him and copying his life, is the most hope-filled adventure that there is.

John Valentine
Holborn, central London
Lent, 2009

1. Learning to do life

Dan and Ria gaze adoringly at the tiny bundle in Ria's arms. Martha was born last night at 11.37. The birth was long but straightforward. Today, it is as if the world has started all over again. They feel so connected to this little girl, so longed for and so prayed for. After seven years of marriage, here she is.

They play games of imagining what she will grow up to be. A concert pianist? Just look at those long fingers! An astronaut? A writer? Will she be famous? Will she ever have children of her own?

The conversation becomes more reflective, more serious. All they really want for Martha is for her to be well and happy. Ria comes from a broken home, where her father was violent and abusive to her mother. It has always been hard for Ria to trust others, especially men. That's part of the reason why her marriage to Dan feels such a miracle to her, such a means of restoring her. Dan's past is colourful, with serial affairs, and issues over drink and drugs – nothing serious, he says, but enough to scare him.

As they think of Martha, they passionately want her to avoid the kind of pain they have both grown up with in different ways. How can Martha live well? What will it take for her to grow up healthy and happy?

Learning by example

'I don't care how hip and cool you are. We all learned to do life from somebody.'

Christian leader Todd Hunter's point is that life is somehow learned. The main way we learn it is through the personal examples of those around us. Nowhere is this clearer, as Dan and Ria know, than with children and their parents. In Martha's early years, and possibly through all her days, the example of her parents will have considerable power in shaping her life, for good and ill.

It is very similar with the Christian life. However hip and cool we may or may not be, we need to learn to do life from another person, and in the case of the Christian, we learn to do life from Jesus. A *Christian* is a Christ in miniature, one who tries to emulate and copy Jesus. The big question for Christians is, 'What would Jesus do if he were living my life here and now?' Discipleship is copying Jesus.

But how do we get to this point?

A matter of image

Jesus shows us what God is like – and what human beings can be
A highly significant phrase in the New Testament is 'the image of God':

'The Son . . . is the image of the invisible God,' Paul writes, 'the firstborn over all creation.'[1]

Paul the apostle is saying the following:

1. In Jesus we see God. God is invisible but Jesus, the Son, shows us God.[2] As the theologian A. M. Ramsay put it, 'God is Christlike and in him is no unChristlikeness at all.' This is one of the foundations of Christian confidence, that in Jesus we really do see what God is like.

2. We also see what *human beings* are like. And Jesus is 'the firstborn over all creation'. Human beings were the pinnacle of all God's creation in the book of Genesis, and pre-eminent among them is Jesus.

The writer of Genesis says: 'Then God said, "Let us make human beings in our image, in our likeness . . . " . . . So God created human beings in his own image, in the image of God he created them; male and female he created them.'[3] Human beings from the first, he says, were designed to be the image, the likeness of God. It's an amazing thing that we human beings are in some sense God-like.

Pause here. The person next to you on the Tube, your class mate, aunt Tilly, your best friend, your worst enemy, even your sister is God-like. All human beings have intrinsic worth, dignity and stature because we reflect God's own image.

And, of course, that includes you. Many in our society see human beings as little more than products of chemistry or social conditioning; the Christian view is that human beings are actually God-like. That means that every person is valuable beyond words, worthy of respect, care, attention.

In an age where self-worth is under constant attack, here is a wonderful corrective. You and I may not be top models or athletes, we may not grace the front pages of newspapers and magazines, we may not be famous, brilliantly clever, admired or revered – indeed it may be just the opposite – but God says we are made to be carriers of his image in the world.

I love the story of the black boy in the Deep South in yester-year, who was told that he was just 'black trash', to which he replied, 'God don't make no trash.'

A defaced image

But how can we hold together Jesus on the one hand as the image of God, and human beings on the other as the image of God?

Sadly, the image of God in human beings has become defaced and distorted, and, some would say, all but irretrievably lost. We have turned in on ourselves and asserted our independence from God. We have forfeited that creation-likeness. Yes, we still carry the image of God, but we are like an old masterpiece that has become covered over with grime and dirt, or even painted over by other artists, so that the original painting is no longer visible except to the most highly trained and attentive of eyes. We need to have the image restored.

And it is in Jesus that we see that image restored. Once again, the likeness of God walks the earth. In Jesus of Nazareth, the image of God can again be seen in all its clarity and startling beauty.

So Jesus is the revelation of God. He is also the revelation of the ultimate human being. This is what it is to be magnificently, gloriously human. This is life as it can be lived by those who are really alive. For those of us who aspire to live our lives to the full, here is how we do it – we try to live like Jesus.

Restoring the image

But how can a grimy painting, undiscovered masterpiece though it may be, come to be restored? How can we, who are crippled by selfishness, pride, anger, hatred and lust, even begin to live

like Jesus? There is such a painful contrast between the perfect human life we see in Jesus and aspects of our own lives.

A powerful contrast

Paul compares Adam and Jesus in another of his letters.[4] He talks of how the first man was the gateway of sin into the world, and that death came into the world on the back of sin. This is powerful language. Sin and death here are powers. Sin kills us. Death reigns or rules over the human race. Condemnation follows – we are in the wrong with God.

By contrast, Jesus is presented to us as living perfectly, not least before God. Adam is the one who was disobedient, while Jesus was obedient. We may chafe at the idea of obedience and find it demeaning, but what Paul is really showing us is how we are going to live and flourish as human beings before God. Adam kicked against God, while Jesus gladly lived in accordance with his Father's will and his ways. Paul may well be thinking of the amazing manner in which Jesus chose to become 'obedient to death – even death on a cross', as Paul describes it elsewhere.[5] Paul encapsulates the contrast: 'For just as through the disobedience of the one man the many were made sinners, so also through the obedience of the one man the many will be made righteous.'[6]

Adam is humanity that has gone wrong. He is the human race with the image of God marred and distorted. This is what it is to be a human being today – trapped in this nexus of sin and death and condemnation, with the odd flashes of the old glory and dignity shining through.

Jesus is the new humanity, which is actually the original ancient humanity restored. What Paul is telling us is that, in and through Jesus Christ, we can all get back to that original splendour.

Think back to Dan and Ria. They still carry some of the old magnificence of God's image, but however good parents they may be, their natural patterns of living which they will pass on to Martha will be the patterns of Adam. What Paul is teaching us here, and what Christian discipleship takes as its starting point, is that there has to be a whole new humanity which somehow comes from within the old humanity, but deals with its huge issues. Martha will need to be part of this new humanity if, in an ultimate sense, she is to be healthy and happy.

So much flows from this.

We can't do it on our own

Fundamentally, we cannot succeed on our own. Ria will never be able to live the fully human life that God had intended. She is trapped in Adam. Paul expresses this darkly but unforgettably by linking sin and death. We were not made to die – that is why we feel it instinctively and viscerally as something alien and profoundly wrong. 'Rage, rage against the dying of the light!' as Dylan Thomas so wonderfully expressed it. We only die because we are 'in Adam' – because humanity has lost its way. Paul is telling us that we cannot find our way back. We cannot breed life out of death. We can never recover the lost ground.

I cannot be a good person. I cannot find this freedom. I cannot truly be myself – not without God, and more specifically, not without Jesus. This reality is deeply unpopular today, but we must face it head on if we are to be truly Christian in our discipleship. So, Christian discipleship is not self-help or self-improvement or turning over a new leaf. It is not finding the answer within myself. It actually begins at the grave – with the crashing realization that I am bound up in a way of living, even a way of being, that will lead inevitably, and without possibility of escape, to death.

Think of it like this. Tragically, family histories repeat themselves. Children of violent, alcoholic parents, statistically, are much more likely themselves to be violent and alcoholic than those who are fortunate enough to grow up in families without such afflictions. It is like that on a global scale. We all belong to the dysfunctional family of the human race. All our instincts, and patterns of thought and behaviour, have been learned deeply within us from those who are fatally infected with a way of life that leads to death. Where can we learn to escape this vicious circle? There are no models of healthy living (in this ultimate sense). In any case, where would we find the inner resources to break free? How can we find something strong enough from within us to overpower death itself? It just cannot be done.

This is not to say, of course, that we are not good people, in the conventional sense, nor that human goodness and kindness are not possible. But it is to say that actually the human race is in trouble – in a deep place from which it will never be able to climb out. This makes me think of going for a walk in the woods, and falling down a huge hole, perhaps some old root system, which feeds into underground caverns. It is dark and far below ground. There is no way of climbing out and, as night falls, cold and hunger will lead eventually to death.

This grim realization is important as our starting point for Christian discipleship. We really need help. We won't find the resources in ourselves. We need someone outside ourselves. That someone is Jesus.

In Jesus, God has done it

Jesus lived the perfect life. He did what no-one else can do. And by doing that, he has created a new future for the human race.

We have seen the contrast between Adam and Jesus. In Paul's thought world, all the present-day tragedies of life ultimately flow from that first man, Adam. Now Adam may have been an amazing person with huge potential for good or ill, but contrast him with Jesus, and it's like putting you or me in goal against David Beckham! Jesus is so much greater and, in and through him, God has more than overturned and reversed the tragic consequences of Adam's life and actions.

In Romans 5, Paul:

- uses the image of *gift*. What we could not do for ourselves, God has given to us in Jesus.

- talks about *grace*. Here that means the loving, freely given power of God to reverse sin and death in human lives.

I love this bit: 'For if, by the trespass of the one man, death reigned through that one man [Adam], how much more will those who receive God's abundant provision of grace and of the gift of righteousness reign in life through the one man, Jesus Christ!'[7] It is all focused in Jesus Christ – God's amazing gift of life, love and a future. And just as Paul talked about death reigning (the power of death before which the human race lay helpless), so now he speaks about humans reigning and ruling. Through Jesus, that image of God – humanity ruling over creation – is restored. We are back where we started, out of the deep hole in the ground. We are fully human again, as God created us to be.

How has Jesus done it? 'Just as one trespass resulted in condemnation for all people, so also one righteous act resulted in justification and life for all.'[8] The trespass, the disobedience, of Adam, led to this whole sorry mess. The one single act of righteousness, 'the obedience of the one man',[9] Jesus Christ, led to life. What is this obedience? Probably a whole life of going God's way, a life of love, a life dedicated to the kingdom of God, but focused ultimately on the 'one righteous act' of laying down his life for the world in obedience to the Father's will. In the midst of so many wrecked lives, what it took was one perfect life of self-sacrificial love, lived out in God's way. And that led to the creation of God's people through the forgiveness of sins, it broke the power of sin over human lives and it broke through the hideous power of the grave – hallelujah!

A new life in Christ

To be Christian then is to move from Adam into Christ. It is a totally different way of being human. It is as if we were on a train heading in one direction (death) and we have changed trains and embarked on a new journey (life).

The Jesus-life is something fresh and new. I think of a man I met in prison. He was young but had already served several years for murder. In prison he had become a Christian and felt himself to be living in a completely different way.

Or I think of the elderly lady who feels that, since becoming a Christian in her late seventies, her life has become somehow multilayered in a way that she never knew before.

Or I think of the banker who says that his life only really began with his conversion to Christ. It is as if he was not alive at all until that great moment.

For many, the feeling may be less powerful and the external change less obvious, but for all of us who are Christians, the truth is no less real. In Christ we have found a way to live that is what we were truly made for.

Living the restored image

There is one final piece of the big-picture jigsaw to put into place. When God restores his image in us in this new Jesus-humanity, he is calling us to work with him for the good of the world.

When God first declares that human beings are to bear his image, he says, 'Let us make human beings in our image, in our likeness, so that they may rule over the fish in the sea and the birds in the sky, over the livestock and all the wild animals, and over all the creatures that move along the ground.'[10]

God makes us in his image to enable us to rule over creation. This is not a mandate for exploitation of the earth and its resources, but it implies a careful and responsible stewardship. Paul picks up this language of ruling in Romans 5: through God's abundant grace in Jesus Christ, we are once more enabled to 'reign in life'.[11] Paul is looking ahead to God's people in the renewed heavens and earth, and he understands it in terms of that original creation mandate finally being fulfilled. Under God's just and gentle rule, human beings will once again (and this time perfectly) bear responsibility for all creation.

This idea of stewardship highlights something that is crucial for our understanding of Christian discipleship. We are restored to our truest selves in Jesus Christ so that we may play a part in God's plan for the whole of creation. When Jesus renews the image of God in humanity, we are restored to have responsibility. We are charged with the fullest flowering of God's creation. So this act of God towards us in Jesus Christ, in all its enormous grace and power, is not ultimately for us alone – it is for the whole human race, for the planet and even the cosmos. God loves all that he has made and refuses to abandon it to decay and destruction. And we have a crucial role to play in his plan of restoration, renewal and wise governance. What a vision!

Landmarks for the journey

I am no great golfer, but I know that it is important to set your feet right when getting ready to drive off down the fairway. The feet set the angle of the shoulders as they address the ball, and the shoulders dictate the direction that the ball takes. Similarly, the picture of the image of God in human beings helps orientate us for the direction that our lives of discipleship will take.

Dan and Ria want the very best for Martha. The Bible's vision for discipleship shows them that in Jesus, and by copying his life, Martha will find a way to be truly and authentically human. She will actually discover her own truest identity as a human being by following Jesus Christ. Christianity is sometimes viewed as something negative and restrictive, but exactly the opposite is the case. Martha will find her truest sense of who she is in Jesus. She will find a way of life that enables her to be free and to flourish. And she will find a way of working with God in his great plan for the world.

As we prepare to look more at what it is like to live out of the restored image of God, we need this radical sense of our own powerlessness, even culpability (we are part of the problem, not the solution). But above all we need the confidence that Paul enjoyed in the sheer abundance of grace that God has given us in Christ.

The words 'how much more' keep recurring throughout his comparison of Jesus with Adam. Jesus is just so much more! More grace, more power, more love, more life! This is not an equal contest between sin and death and the power of God in Jesus Christ! We shall 'reign in life through the one man, Jesus Christ'.[12]

2. Becoming human

Kate is in her final year at school. She is acting in the school play. It is the last night and all has gone amazingly well. The cast are just getting changed after the final performance. There are cards going round which they are all signing, giving messages of thanks and love. There is music blaring, good and loud. It seems to express the confidence, the sense of achievement, the joy, of what they have all done together. The cast go round the room, hugging one another. There is lots of laughter, and actually there are a few tears as well.

Kate has loved the play. It has almost given her access into another world. She has thrown herself into it, and it has been amazing to discover so much creativity within herself. Rehearsals were great. There was the thrill of putting something together, of discovering the beauty of the language of the play, and a meaning that seemed to spring into life from the page as they improvised, and then went to the words. There was a clear feeling of camaraderie between the actors, the director and the crew. They felt like a band of brothers and sisters. Then the performances amazed her. She was not prepared for the sense of power of communicating with a live audience. And although it may sound naff, there was also the sense that this was an offering for them, something of love and wisdom which could alter their lives if they could receive it.

Kate feels that this experience of the play has changed her. It has given her a new sense of self-confidence. There has been self-discovery as she has found out things about herself. She never knew that she could be a key player in a team operation like this, and she has revelled in the experience. She has discovered that she has something to say, and that there is exhilaration in saying it. The team have become friends. She wants to use the word 'love', although it does not feel like the usual way in which the word is used.

There is of course a tinge of sadness for her on this last night. Along with the triumph, there is a sense of loss. It is all over now. Will anything else in life ever match it?

The glory of God is a human being fully alive

Sometimes we get the idea from our culture that to be a Christian is all about self-denial, even self-negation. Actually, the goal of Christian discipleship is the rediscovery of nothing less than our true humanity (the image of God).

Irenaeus was a second-century theologian. He expresses a wonderful truth: 'the glory of God is a human being fully alive.' He talks about the idea of 'recapitulation':

When [Christ] was incarnate and became a human being, he recapitulated in himself the long history of the human race, obtaining salvation for us, so that we might regain in Jesus Christ what we had lost in Adam, that is being in the image and likeness of God.[1]

He is arguing that Jesus came to relive the human story, to recreate the human race, rescuing us from the self-destructive patterns of living we had got into by rejecting God. Irenaeus gives us a vision of Christianity which is all about being fully and gloriously alive. It is about the affirmation, not the denial, of our humanity.

This begs the question of what it means to be a human being. How do human beings work, and work well?

I find Kate's experience fascinating. She has discovered being in the school play exhilarating and affirming. She has grown in self-understanding and self-confidence. She has made friends, found community and communicated something of wisdom and value to others. She doesn't want anything of this experience to be lost. She wants her life to develop and be formed by such experiences. We could say that she has found an experience of being 'fully alive'. Should we expect to find areas of considerable overlap between Kate's experience of the play and our own of Christian discipleship? I think so.

Some of the deepest experiences of my own life have come from shared experiences of Christian service. When I was twenty, a group of us who were actors and singers conducted a week-long mission amid the beauty of several villages in Wiltshire. We had a brilliant time, the lives of some people from the area were changed forever and one member of the team went on to marry the local farmer. For me, an unlooked-for benefit was the closeness of the friendships within the team.

In our church, we run the Alpha course as a rolling programme. Like others such as Christianity Explored, this course is highly effective in introducing people to Jesus Christ in a natural and non-threatening way. Again, one of the side effects is that lifelong friendships develop as the course goes on. On one Alpha course, two old friends brought along their girlfriends, neither of whom was a Christian. Both girls came to Christ and have now gone on to marry their respective boyfriends. I was privileged to be involved in both weddings, and these couples continue to be some of the closest friends of my wife Catherine and myself.

Again, in our church, every year we run something we call 'WAVE'. This is an intensive period of social-action projects, when volunteers demonstrate the love of God in practical ways to our local community. The projects are focused on particular practical needs (painting a flat, tidying an estate, building a shelter, planting a garden), but the longer-lasting impact is often one of friendship. There is a real sense of camaraderie on the teams, and often a bond between team members and those who so bravely invite them into their homes to decorate.

I find it helpful to reflect on these experiences. They say something to me, not just about what *Christians* do, but about what it means to be a *human being*. If being human and being a disciple of Jesus Christ are parallel, these experiences will tell me something important about both.[2]

Reflect on those times when you have felt most powerfully and wonderfully alive. Don't put any value judgments on the experiences, simply note them. Such experiences can be big or small, from your wedding day and the birth of your children to winning a game of football; they might be walking on a beach, attending an amazing gig in a bar or painting a picture.

Please hold in your mind your examples and the ones I have given, and let's turn to some biblical insights into what it is to be a human being, before returning to our life experiences.

The heart of humanity: body, mind and spirit

A good place to start is when Jesus, in conversation with one of the teachers of the law, says that the most important commandment is to 'love the Lord your God with all your heart and with all your soul and with all your mind and with all your strength'.[3] Without wanting to draw too-large conclusions from one text, it seems that Jesus is giving us a thumbnail sketch of how human beings work best. We have centres of personality (the heart), centres of life, particularly as they relate to God (the soul), centres of thought (the mind) and centres of energy (all our strength). All of these come into play when directed to God in devotion and love. Clearly, the point is that these various centres together add up to what it is to be a total human being: Jesus' point is that God deserves all our love, from every facet of our beings and personality.

Body

How striking that Jesus includes 'strength' as one of the ways in which human beings are to love God. The physical is just as much part of a life of worship as the more overtly 'spiritual' part of humanity.

This is an emphasis picked up by Paul. He encourages us to think of our bodies as being firmly within the ambit of the life of discipleship: 'Therefore, I urge you, brothers and sisters, in view of God's mercy, to offer your bodies as a living sacrifice, holy and pleasing to God – this is true worship.'[4]

Paul is applying an Old Testament model (bringing sacrifices to God) into a New Testament context. He is saying, 'Bring your bodies to God as your worship.'

He has already given an explanation in his letter to the church in Rome: 'Do not offer any part of yourself to sin as an instrument of wickedness, but rather offer yourselves to God as those who have been brought from death to life: and offer every part of yourself to him as an instrument of righteousness.'[5] This seems alien to us and our modern understanding, but Paul is saying that the body has considerable power over the way we live our lives. If we learn to present each part of our bodies to God for his purposes, then we will be on the way to living lives of holiness – that is, fully human lives.

There is something here about a deliberate presenting of one's whole self to God, and the realization that we must take our physicality seriously. The Christian faith insists not that we are most truly ourselves when we are most 'spiritual', but rather that we are bodies and spirits and minds all bound together. When we die, ultimately our spirits will not go off to heaven, released from our bodies which are thankfully left behind. No; rather, we shall be resurrected, so that body and spirit together will be reconstituted in glory. Our bodies are just as much us as are our spirits.

I read of one distinguished Christian leader who every morning in his prayers offers each part of his body to the Lord for his service. He prays that the Lord Jesus will take his hands and use them for good, his mouth to speak words of life and truth, and so on. This is a wonderful outworking of Paul's teaching.

Discipleship recognizes that we are bodies, as well as minds and spirits. We must think about our physical appetites. We need to consider, on the one hand, the impact on our lives of being tired, unfit or ill and, on the other, the good our bodies can do to others and ourselves. And we must reckon with what it is to be physical creatures in a physical world that is not what it was initially created to be.

We must look at routine and habit too. Certainly, we know the power of habitual action. As soon as we have done something once, it is easier to do it again. This is true in learning to play tennis, just as much as in taking drugs. The repeated action of throwing the ball into the air in just the right way and to the right height can be learned by the body. When we practise scales for hours and hours as we learn the violin, we are teaching our fingers certain patterns that can be reproduced when we are playing a piece of music.

Paul says that there are aspects of the Christian life that are like that. Teach ourselves to be human. How? By teaching our bodies certain patterns. What might they be? Negatively, not to

learn habits of wickedness (whether illicit sex, or sleep depriv-
ation, or eating too much or too little or too fast, or whatever it
might be). Positively, to learn the habits of being available to God
and to his service (showing honour through our posture when
we pray, getting up early on occasions to pray, or being physically
involved in serving others, maybe through shopping or gardening
for elderly neighbours, or moving chairs in church).

Paul talks elsewhere of mastering our bodies.[6] There's the
sheer energy required to live a full-on life for Jesus Christ. It's
hard work and will make demands on us physically, as well
as emotionally and in every other way. However, it is important
to say though that this is not the kind of masochism that has
been popular in certain times in the history of the church. The
body is to be mastered, yes, but never tortured.

Mind

Just as Jesus calls us to love God with all our minds, Paul also
alerts us to the importance of the mind in Christian discipleship
when he says, 'Do not conform to the pattern of this world, but
be transformed by the renewing of your mind. Then you will be
able to test and approve what God's will is – his good, pleasing
and perfect will.'[7] A change of behaviour (not conforming to an
external norm) is generated by a mental change (the renewal of
our minds).

He makes the same point in several places. In Ephesians, he
writes, 'So I tell you this, and insist on it in the Lord, that you
must no longer live as the Gentiles do, in the futility of their
thinking.'[8] In Romans he explains, 'For although they [human
beings] knew God, they neither glorified him as God nor gave
thanks to him, but their thinking became futile and their foolish
hearts were darkened.'[9] He uses the same phrase in both letters:
'the futility of their thinking' – an empty, useless way of looking
at the world, which leads to an empty, useless, ineffective life.
The context of both passages is that our attitude to God will
determine how we look at the world. Once we think certain

thoughts about God, there will inevitably be consequences in how we lead our lives. That is why, in Romans at least, the context of these remarks is worship. If our praise of God has as its starting point what he is truly like, then we will have a right view of the world. And if we substitute false gods from the created world (whether from our human sphere or any other), then we will lose our full dignity as those who bear the image of the glorious true God.

So, in biblical terms, when we talk about the mind in discipleship, we are talking not about cleverness, but rather about thinking true thoughts concerning God. The mind is the place where idolatry is located in the human personality. We end up being like what we worship. Our lives will be shaped by what we fix our thoughts on.

I remember once, when I was working in a solicitor's office, meeting a man who told me with great pride that his whole life was about making money. He was very good at it, and, in his own words, thought about nothing else. It was chilling.

Later in his letter to the Romans, Paul sums up the place of the mind: 'Those who live according to the sinful nature have their minds set on what that nature desires; but those who live in accordance with the Spirit have their minds set on what the Spirit desires. The mind controlled by the sinful nature is death, but the mind controlled by the Spirit is life and peace.'[10] In Philippians, he broadens the point and gives us a beautiful injunction to fill our minds with good things: 'Finally, brothers and sisters, whatever is true, whatever is noble, whatever is right, whatever is pure, whatever is lovely, whatever is admirable – if anything is excellent or praiseworthy – think about such things.'[11]

So, the mind is going to be the engine room of so much Christian discipleship. This does not mean that we must all become highly cerebral people. But it does mean that what we do think about will have a powerful effect on our lives. Most especially, thinking good, true and accurate thoughts about God will shape our Christian living. And those thoughts will have considerable power. The renewing of our minds will lead to freedom from running with the crowd, and into all the freedom and joy of God's perfect and pleasing ways for human living and flourishing.

Spirit

Jesus encourages us to love God with all our heart and soul too. From our point of view, the inner focus is very significant. Jesus gives us an understanding of how our outward-facing lives spring from what goes on within.

'The heart' is the Bible's shorthand for this inner life, this volitional centre of human personality and being. The book of Proverbs says, 'Above all else, guard your heart, for everything you do flows from it.'[12] It becomes a synonym for sincerity when Jesus says that you are to 'forgive a brother or sister from your heart',[13] something that comes from the deepest part of us. Jesus pronounces a blessing on 'the pure in heart, for they will see God'[14] – a picture of singleness of mind or an uncompromised focus on God.

Sadly, but realistically, we get a picture of the human heart, which is in need of radical surgery. 'For from within, out of your hearts, come evil thoughts, sexual immorality, theft, murder, adultery, greed, malice, deceit, lewdness, envy, slander, arrogance and folly. All these evils come from inside and defile you,'[15] says Jesus. Jeremiah says something very similar: 'The heart is deceitful above all things and beyond cure.'[16]

This means that discipleship without this radical surgery is not possible. Jesus, quoting Isaiah, says, 'These people honour me with their lips, but their hearts are far from me.'[17] We have a problem, which is beyond our power to fix.

But it's not beyond God and his power. Christian salvation can be viewed from two aspects.

- On the one hand, it is us getting into Jesus (what we were thinking about in the last chapter). We are in Adam, and we need to get into this whole new humanity, which is known as in Jesus, or in Christ. We change trains, we get into another river, we move across into this whole new stream of life and living – the renewed human race in Jesus.

- On the other hand, we need Jesus to get into us. We don't just need to bring our lives into the flow of his life, we also need to get his life into our lives. We need Jesus, by his Spirit, to live his life in and through us.

One of my favourite songs, which is supposed to be a children's song, but expresses an all-too-adult truth powerfully, goes like this:

I need a new heart
A new clean heart
A heart that won't fight
When I try to do what's right.
I need my spirit restored
So I can follow you, Lord.
Lord, help me be strong
Lord, help me be strong.[18]

And a new heart and a restored spirit is what God gives to us in Christ. Ezekiel prophesies, in God's name: 'I will give you a new heart and put a new spirit in you; I will remove from you your heart of stone and give you a heart of flesh. And I will put my Spirit in you and move you to follow my decrees and be careful to keep my laws.'[19] Paul tells us that 'God . . . works in you to will and to act in order to fulfil his good purpose'.[20] This is what lies behind Jesus' famous words, 'You must be born again.'[21] We need, not a new start, but a new nature, a nature regenerated by the Holy Spirit. God is remaking us from the inside out.

This is where we start from in our understanding of discipleship and of being human: a new heart. Andrei Platanov, presumably writing about the Russian Revolution, said, 'Busy remaking the world, man forgot to remake himself.'[22] Jesus remakes a new world by remaking human hearts one by one. Paul says: 'If anyone is in Christ, the new creation has come: the old has gone, the new is here!'[23]

So a biblical view of Christian discipleship is that we need to be remade on the inside before the outside (our behaviour, our actions, our speech, even our secret attitudes and prejudices). When we are changed from the inside out, then we can lastingly and authentically be brought into line with Jesus and his ways and purposes. On the one hand, we are like a stream which has become polluted – we need to be totally cleansed at source. And on the other hand we are like a glove – we need the presence of a hand within us if we are to have the power to lift the glass of water beside us. To live the Christian life in all its fullness, we need both rebirth and renewal.

What does this mean for you and me in practice? It means that we must start all attempts at living the God-life with deep humility. We cannot do it. We need to be remade. We need him, through Jesus and the Holy Spirit, to live this life in us. To be fully human, we need the ultimate human, Jesus, to live his life in and through us.

Socialization

Another piece of the matrix is that, for us as human beings, keeping good company makes a huge difference.

I wonder how many of your examples of feeling most fully alive involved other people? Our different personalities will influence our choices, so there will be examples of having climbed a mountain and stared alone across amazing scenery, or maybe examples of individual achievement or suffering. But I reckon that many of your examples will be shared experiences. It seems that for us as human beings, many of our greatest moments are often those spent in company with others.

This should not surprise us at a number of levels.

- In terms of the narrative of the Bible, it is important to God to have numbers of people together. The covenant was with Israel, 'I will take you as my own people, and I will be your God,'[24] not with individuals. It was through the descendants of Abraham that God would display his glory in the world, not through one or two 'superstars'. And the New Testament presents the church as the chief arena for God's presence and activity in the world.

- Christianity teaches us that God is the Trinity: he is three persons in one godhead. He is community in himself. That is how we can say that God is love, not just loving.

- Several pictures of the renewed creation emphasize harmony in creation and community. So Isaiah can talk about the wolf living with the lamb, the leopard lying down with the goat, little children playing with calves and lions.[25] Zechariah sees old men and women sitting happily in the streets with boys and girls playing all round them.[26] One of the word pictures of the Old Testament that Jesus seems to have been particularly fond of is of the great Messianic feast: men and women celebrating at a huge party with the Messiah.[27] And the end of the Bible paints two complementary pictures of heaven as the Holy City, the new Jerusalem and as the Garden of Eden (where the first human beings lived together in fellowship with God and with one another).[28]

God has a plan for people together. In our individualistic age this is hard to grasp, but actually our experiences affirm it. Why did the experience of being in the school play have such a powerful effect on Kate? Well, it had a lot to do with the play (it must have been Shakespeare!), but mainly it was the shared experience of being involved with others in a great and worthwhile project. So it was in my experience of the Alpha course and those from our church involved in the WAVE activities. So it is with going to football matches, being part of a band, having a good meal out with friends, experiencing a companionable family evening, enjoying a shared joke with others or being caught up in wonderful music at a concert.

And the quality of the socialization will affect the experience and have power to shape it. It amazes me how two institutions or organizations involved in the same line of work can have such different cultures. Schools in the same city or town can be as different as chalk and cheese. Churches can have their own distinctive cultures. We create and shape the way life is done by our interactions together. Paul can quote a pretty brisk proverb to this effect, 'Bad company corrupts good character',[29] because it sums up wisdom from elsewhere throughout the Bible.

All this has far-reaching implications for us as we consider Christian discipleship: we see it works much better in the company of like-minded others. Socialization is very important. My default picture of discipleship or of holiness is usually individuals praying on their own. I think that the fuller biblical picture is of many people together, encouraging one another, relating together and enjoying it, engaged in some common activity that focuses them on God and what he wants to be done in the world. They share a vision and have embarked on a journey of discovery as together they follow God in this world and into the next. It is so much more fun than being on our own, not least because it is so in line with our humanity. We simply enjoy life more together with other people. We are back to where we started, as human beings fully alive.

Human beings fully alive

In the last chapter, we thought about how God had done nothing less than remake humanity in Jesus Christ. To be a Christian is to have moved over from being 'in Adam' to being 'in Christ'.

To be Christian is to be put into this wonderful stream of living differently.

So we see the other side of the coin. Not only are we now 'in Christ' but Christ is also in us.[30] Jesus, through the power of the Holy Spirit, comes to live his perfect human life in and through us. As he does this, he renews our essential humanity from deep within. As we follow him, as his disciples, we shall find out that there is no part of our humanity (our hearts, minds or bodies) that is unaffected.

Not only has Jesus made possible a new way of living, he has enabled us to live in this way. We can be so glad that to be Christians is truly to be ourselves at our most alive.

3. Copying Jesus

Matt has just turned thirty-five. He has a busy and demanding job as a teacher. He is good at his job and likes the children and the teaching. He does not like the growing administrative and managerial sides to the job, however. He tends to work himself to exhaustion and then collapse at half-term, and for the first three days of each holiday.

He is single and does not have many really close friends. He is intelligent and charming, but battles with insecurities and issues of self-confidence. He longs to be married and has periods of panicking that he will go through life single. He struggles with pornography, anger, binge drinking and eating.

Matt has been a Christian since university days. He loved those early exhilarating times, and was a regular at pretty much every prayer meeting and Christian event. University passed in a blur of Christian activities, and, as he looks back, Matt regrets that he did not take more advantage of the other cultural and social opportunities.

Since then, his faith has had periodic flashes of the same intensity, followed by increasingly long periods in the doldrums. Sometimes he has months when he does not go to church, until either guilt or fresh enthusiasm drives him back. He finds that he is just not that keen any more. He is really interested in girls and in finding a way of managing the more irrational aspects of his character and personality. These frighten him more and more, but he does not seem to be finding answers to these deeper issues from his faith or his Christian friends. Church seems so irrelevant to his daily working life and the struggles which increasingly dominate.

One day, he is sitting in church next to someone he vaguely knows. To Matt's embarrassment, this man starts to cry during the worship. Matt asks if he is OK. They begin to talk, and their conversation carries on in the pub after church. To Matt's amazement, this other man's story pretty much exactly replicates his own. The two men agree to meet up to talk more and pray for each other. For both men this could be the start of something really important.

Matt's story is far from unique. In fact, it is a part-fictional weaving together of countless conversations I have had with men and women in church life over the past ten years, mixed up with some of my own experiences too. Part of what is so crippling in such stories is the sense of being alone and being the only one, a freak totally unlike all the other happy and holy Christians all around. It is so liberating to discover that actually this story is more the norm than the exception. For all of us, discipleship does not come easily or naturally. It is a struggle, and one which we frequently feel we are losing.

In succeeding chapters, we shall be looking at what are called the spiritual disciplines: Christian practices of prayer, Bible reading and so on. Before we get there, however, this chapter aims to provide a context and an overall picture of the main spiritual disciplines.

The context – whole-life discipleship

Let me say this right at the beginning. Our aim is not to become super-Christians, but to live the whole of our lives in a Christian way. We do not want to become brilliant at praying, without it affecting how we conduct our relationships. It would be such a shame to become experts in the Bible, but still to be ruled by anger or our physical appetites. No, the vision that the Bible offers us is of a whole life, beautifully integrated around following Jesus. Praying, Bible reading, going to church and so on are all parts of that, and make the whole possible. A holy and good person is not defined as someone who prays a lot or who reads the Bible every day. Discipleship is being a human being fully alive. Discipleship is living life the way Jesus would live my life were he in my shoes. The spiritual disciplines are what enable us to live this kind of life, the life we have always wanted.

So what we are thinking about together is not how to pray as an end in itself. It is rather trying to discover how our daily, real lives can be resourced by prayer, so that, in all we do, we can somehow carry out lives that reflect the image of God and glorify him. Think of Paul saying, 'Whatever you do, whether in word or deed, do it all in the name of the Lord Jesus, giving thanks to God the Father through him.'[1]

John Ortberg, in his wonderful book *The Life You've Always Wanted*, in a very amusing and illuminating passage, reflects on what it would look like to go shopping in Jesus' name, to drive in his name, or to get up or go to sleep in his name. Discipleship is how the whole of our lives can be Christian – that is to say, how our lives can speak of Jesus, be fully human, fully alive, and so glorify God by reflecting his image in the world. The spiritual disciplines are what make this kind of life possible. They are the means of getting the life of Jesus into our lives, and so enabling us to live in this kind of way.

I hope this strikes at the heart of much of the neurosis and the unhappiness that can spring up whenever we start to talk about prayer and Bible reading. Please put aside all false guilt at this point. You are not a disaster as a Christian if you are not praying regularly, or if you find reading the Bible difficult, or if your attendance at church is patchy to say the least. These things are all there to be a kind of scaffolding around the beautiful building that lies at the heart of being a Christian, that is, how you live your life in and with Jesus, to the glory of God the Father.

So for Matt, discipleship will mean looking at the big picture of his life. On the one hand, he is being driven by inner demons. And on the other, his life is increasingly disconnected from God. The journey for him is how to reconnect with God in such a way that he can find the resources to understand himself and his situation, and to disarm the power of those issues which are currently controlling his life. He will want to find spiritual disciplines that work for him in effectively channelling the life of Jesus into his life, so that the fear of singleness is calmed, his work-life balance is addressed, and his needs for comfort, communication, friendship and intimacy are met in healthy ways, so that he does not need to have recourse to abusing food and drink, or to retreat into the fantasy world of pornography. He will want to find a pattern of praying and living that works for him. He is looking for patterns of discipleship that are not driven by guilt. He is searching for ways of living that lead him into the love and freedom that Jesus came to bring.

For Matt, focusing on his life, rather than on what increasingly feels like a treadmill of prayer and Bible reading, could see joy come back into his relationship with God. It could reconnect God into every area of his life, and, paradoxically, open up more prayer and Bible reading than he has known for years.

The most important thing – discipleship is copying Jesus

Here is the heart of the thesis of this book: Christian discipleship is following Jesus. We can be even more precise: it is copying Jesus, trying to model our lives on his life. When Paul says, 'Follow my example, as I follow the example of Christ,'[2] he means that he has been copying or imitating Christ, and he encourages the Christians in Corinth to do the same.

The logic is this: Jesus shows to us what it is to live the perfect human life. In order to live our lives to the very best, we model our living on his. To be human beings fully alive, we try (with the help of the Holy Spirit) to live in the same way as Jesus, the ultimate and perfect human being. The heart of discipleship is to move this from the level of good theology into the arena of our daily living.

We can see this pattern in the way that Jesus trained his disciples. For instance, on the night before he died, he did what only slaves would have done in that time by washing the feet of his disciples. Then he said, 'Now that I, your Lord and Teacher, have washed your feet, you also should wash one another's feet. I have set you an example that you should do as I have done for you.'[3] We see the pattern again in the way that 'he appointed twelve [apostles] that they might be with him and that he might send them out to preach and to have authority to drive out demons'.[4] The order is very instructive: first, to be with Jesus and, presumably, to see what he did, then, second, to go and do it for themselves. We see the outworking of this pattern in the way that Matthew in his Gospel shows Jesus, first modelling, then instructing, and then commissioning the disciples to do the same things as he did. First, we read that 'Jesus went throughout Galilee, teaching in their synagogues, proclaiming the good news of the kingdom, and healing every disease and illness among the people',[5] and later Jesus instructs the disciples, 'As you go, proclaim this message: "The kingdom of heaven has come near." Heal the sick, raise the dead, cleanse those who have leprosy, drive out demons.'[6] When Peter, in the Acts of the Apostles, is called to the bedside of the recently deceased Dorcas, he finds the room full of weeping relatives and friends. He sends them out of the room, prays, tells her to get up, then takes her by the hand to help her up.[7] Where did he learn how to do that? Well, when Jesus was summoned to the bedside of a little girl who had just died, he found the place overrun with weeping relatives and friends, he sent them out, he took the little girl by the hand and told her to get up,[8] exactly what Peter did years later. Jesus had not let anyone follow him there except Peter, James and John. He was training them, so that they would know what to do – they would copy him, imitate him, follow his example.

This call to copy Jesus is true in the realm of prayer too (more about this in chapter 5). The disciples saw Jesus praying, and wanted to pray like him. He gave them the pattern of what we now call the Lord's prayer. 'One day Jesus was praying in a certain place. When he finished, one of his disciples said to him, "Lord, teach us to pray . . . " He said to them, "When you pray, say: 'Father . . . '"'[9] Jesus was revolutionary in addressing God as Father, and the early church unanimously addressed God as Father. They prayed as Jesus prayed. They learned by copying him.

This is the most important principle of discipleship. The big picture (we recover the lost image and likeness of God in Jesus, who is that true likeness and image – the human being fully alive) is focused into the real, daily habits and actions of Jesus, the truly human one. And we find our true humanity, our authentic discipleship, in copying him, doing what he did, praying the way he prayed, living the way he lived. Discipleship is patterning our lives on the pattern of his life.

Of course, there are certain things which were unique to him in his vocation as the Son of God. We are not called to bear the sins of the world on the cross, for instance. And it is something of a moot point whether or not Jesus could do certain things that we cannot, by virtue of his divinity and our flawed humanity. And, of course, we will need to take the principles that lay behind Jesus' practices and translate them into the idiom of our modern, contemporary lives. But the core of it is true and strong: to live the free and authentic human life of Christian discipleship, we copy Jesus Christ.

This means that the Gospels will be very important for us. We will read them carefully to learn how Jesus actually lived his life. But the rest of the Scriptures too will show us the Jesus life, whether by prophecy or typology in the Old Testament,[10] or by fulfilment, emulation and the inspiration of the Spirit in the rest of the New. How interesting that Luke began the Acts of the Apostles by saying, 'In my former book [his Gospel], Theophilus, I wrote about all that Jesus began to do and to teach . . . ',[11] with the clear implication that it is Jesus who continues to do and teach things in volume 2.

Copying Jesus' life – how?

In the rest of this chapter we shall look at what spiritual disciplines Jesus used to fund his own discipleship.[12] What were the practices that Jesus embraced which enabled him to live the perfect life? I shall try to keep them at the level of principles, so that we can each adapt them to our own lives, personalities and situations. This is not 'one size fits all': we shall each need to adapt the specifics to our own lives.

Jesus' practices can be grouped under the following headings: worship, study, solitude and service. This is how he resourced his life, and this is how we too can live fully human lives.

Worship
There is nothing flashy or showy in Jesus' commitment to worship, but it is everywhere. It is like the proverbial iceberg,

occasionally visible above the surface of the water but going down hundreds and hundreds of metres out of sight.

This is why we find Jesus in the synagogue on the Sabbath day 'as was his custom'.[13] We find him praying on his own for long periods of time, especially at important times such as when choosing the Twelve,[14] facing grief at the violent death of his cousin, John the Baptist,[15] wrestling with the anguish of Gethsemane[16] or praying with the disciples before his arrest.[17] There are spontaneous outbursts of praise,[18] and there is the telling detail that, even under the huge pressure of his impending arrest and murder, Jesus and the disciples still manage to sing a hymn.[19]

We see in Jesus a life that is conformed to the will of his Father in action and orientation, as well as in the practice of prayer and worship. 'Very truly I tell you,' he says, 'the Son can do nothing by himself; he can do only what he sees his Father doing, because whatever the Father does the Son also does.'[20] Gethsemane was the culmination of a life lived in loving, joyful obedience to the Father: a life of worship.

Here is something of prime importance – Jesus shows us that to live the fully human life, we start with God. It seems such a paradox, but to be fully ourselves, we begin by looking away from ourselves. As worship of God becomes something foundational to the orientation of our lives, we come into full human joy and freedom.

I remember a wise friend telling me once that sometimes the way to deal with a particular issue or worry in my life was by focusing on something else. As I did this, I would find the perspective to deal with the original concern. Jesus shows us that this principle is true on a much broader canvas. We discover the essence of true and authentic humanness in relationship with God. Our natural assumption is that we find ourselves by focusing on ourselves or our human environment. The leap of faith that was Jesus' earthly life is to show us that in abandoning ourselves in praise and worship and trust to God, that is how we most truly find ourselves. We lose our lives in order to find them.[21]

In the Bible the word 'worship' means much more than singing songs and hymns in church, although these are certainly not the least part of it. Worship is a whole life lived in gratitude to, and in dependence on, God. To walk through our lives in the company of God is to be like the original Adam and Eve. The first principle of Jesus' life serves to create in us an orientation in life that looks first to God, and only then to ourselves and others. Our hearts are, as it were, always turned up towards God in praise, thanksgiving and prayer, wherever we are and whatever we are doing. We find ways of offering everything that we do first to God in praise and gratitude.

How we do this will vary with each one of us. The fundamental principle is that our lives are *for* God. We live for the praise of his glory – not the other way round! The position of the Christian heart is one of worship to God.

Paradoxically, it is as we do this that we discover a joy and a freedom that we did not know before. We find ourselves in our proper place within the whole order of things, and this gives us a security and self-understanding that are greatly liberating.

Study
The second feature of Jesus's earthly life is study. It is apparent from his conversations with others just how well he knew what we now call the Old Testament Scriptures. His mind was deeply trained in the Bible and in other aspects of life too.

This is not to imply that Jesus was some kind of egghead, but rather that he was immersed in the Hebrew Scriptures. Jesus' whole life was shaped by and founded on them: from the time when he was only twelve years old and amazed everyone by 'his understanding and his answers'[22] to those fraught debates with the Sadducees and Pharisees in the temple courts in the last days of his life, when he confounded them by his use of the Scriptures;[23] from his debate with the devil, when he answered all his temptations with quotations from the beginning of Deuteronomy (had he been meditating on those passages?)[24] to the cry of dereliction from the cross, itself a quotation from one of the Psalms;[25] from the framing of his mission in terms of a prophecy from Isaiah[26] to his self-understanding as the Son of Man prophesied by Ezekiel and Daniel[27] and the Suffering Servant of Isaiah.[28]

It is striking too how Jesus used the categories of the Bible to frame the way he looked at and understood how God was acting in the world. The story of the people of Israel, especially the exodus; the wisdom, word, Spirit and glory of God; the promised renewal of all things; the shepherd leadership of God's people: all of these underpinned the way that Jesus thought about things, his view of God's big plan for the world, and how he could be part of it.

Jesus was clearly also someone who reflected deeply on life. His teaching is original, and framed in such a way as to hook into people's minds and memories. His parables were usually taken from the natural world, maybe as he and the disciples were walking together in the countryside. Jesus 'studied' in this sense too.

Jesus shows us by example just how significant the mind is in the shaping of a human life. What we think about will affect the kind of person that we become. When it comes to worship and the Christian life, it is crucial to think right thoughts about God. Jesus' thought-world, self-understanding and vocation all came from meditation on Scripture.

Again, how we take this on board will vary greatly according to our individual personalities and learning styles. But what Jesus shows us is that a fully human life, lived in fellowship with God and to his praise and glory, will be one that is deeply shaped and formed by a familiarity with Scripture, having a mind that thinks deeply and truly about the world.

This is not about returning to school or living in a library! The danger is that we make Christian discipleship something unduly cerebral or academic. It is not. But it is a life that takes seriously what we put into our minds, and insists that the Bible will occupy a primary place. We all think that certain people or sources of information are more important than others when it comes to how we live. For us Christians trying to follow Jesus, the Bible will hold a supreme place in our devotion.

Solitude

When we come to copying him, solitude is one of the most striking features of Jesus' life. He was frequently alone and seeking out opportunities to be on his own or away from crowds.

Here are some examples, following through Mark's Gospel.

- 'Very early in the morning, while it was still dark, Jesus got up, left the house and went off to a solitary place, where he prayed.'[29]
- 'Jesus withdrew with his disciples to the lake.'[30]
- 'Jesus went up on a mountainside and called to him those he wanted, and they came to him.'[31]
- 'That day when evening came, he said to his disciples, "Let us go over to the other side." Leaving the crowd behind, they took him along, just as he was, in the boat.'[32]
- 'Then, because so many people were coming and going that they did not even have a chance to eat, he said to them, "Come with me by yourselves to a quiet place and get some rest." So they went away by themselves in a boat to a solitary place.'[33]
- 'After leaving them, he went up on a mountainside to pray.'[34]
- 'Jesus left that place and went to the vicinity of Tyre. He entered a house and did not want anyone to know it.'[35]
- 'After six days Jesus took Peter, James and John with him and led them up a high mountain, where they were all alone.'[36]

- 'They left that place and passed through Galilee. Jesus did not want anyone to know where they were, because he was teaching his disciples.'[37]
- 'Jesus entered Jerusalem and went into the temple courts. He looked around at everything, but since it was already late, he went out to Bethany with the Twelve.'[38]
- 'They went to a place called Gethsemane, and Jesus said to his disciples, "Sit here while I pray." He took Peter, James and John along with him.' (And he goes 'a little further', so that he can pray on his own.)[39]
- '"Don't be alarmed," [the young man] said. "You are looking for Jesus the Nazarene, who was crucified. He has risen! He is not here. But go, tell his disciples and Peter, 'He is going ahead of you into Galilee.'"'[40]

Jesus' efforts to find peace and solitude are all the more striking given the constant pressure from the crowds. This peace and solitude was clearly at a premium for him. He uses it for himself, and also for the disciples. Sometimes it is for rest, sometimes for prayer, sometimes for uninterrupted instruction. He uses special places: for example, Bethany assumes great importance in the last week of his life. And isn't it especially evocative that the pattern continues even after the resurrection?

How we find solitude, and for what lengths of time, will be determined by our circumstances and temperaments. For anyone taking the life of Jesus as their model though, times of solitude are non-negotiable. (We shall examine this further in chapter 5.)

Service

Jesus highlights service in his teaching, and exemplifies it in his actions: 'The Son of Man did not come to be served, but to serve, and to give his life as a ransom for many.'[41] 'I am among you as one who serves.'[42] And he washes the feet of his disciples. The greatest act of service is the giving of his life for the world on the cross of Calvary.

We see it, all so unaffected, in the way Jesus is available to people. He is in the street going somewhere, and yet stops for a chance encounter with the woman with the flow of blood, or the tax collector in the tree. He has time for children, for questions, for impertinences, for accusations, for desperate pleas. His own agenda is given over to God, and because of that to others God may send. He is not always reactive,[43] but whether in conversation or travel or the use of time or the resetting of an agenda, he shows an astonishing flexibility and a willingness to put others before himself. The most striking example for me is when he takes the disciples away because he is exhausted. He has just heard about the death of John the Baptist – a time of great personal need for him – yet he still has compassion on the crowds that follow him, so he teaches and feeds them.[44] Amazing.

The Red and Dead Seas are very different: the one is fresh and beautiful, teeming with life; the other, so salty that nothing lives there, and very unpleasant even to swim in. The difference is that the Dead Sea has no flow at all, no input or output. So too with the Christian life. If we are not taking in and also giving out, we get spiritually stagnant.

The spirituality of Jesus bears this out. He resources the fully-alive human life, with an emphasis, both in word and deed, on service. To be alive, we need to be regularly and actively helping others.

This means that we will want to be involved in some form of service, both in the church and outside it. Jesus' point is a fundamental one: discipleship involves not just work for its own sake, but service, something humble. We are aiming for something that is about others, not about us. We are attacking pride, selfishness and laziness, and hopefully doing some good too.

Again, isn't it striking how Jesus lived the fully human life by centring himself on others and putting their needs before his own? Fully to find ourselves, once more we find the principle that we have to lose ourselves.

Developing the fully human life

Matt is facing many challenges and he does not feel that his Christian faith has much connection with the issues that are driving and dominating him. What Jesus offers to Matt is a vision for being fully and joyfully himself. The key will not be to focus on the various issues and pressures he is feeling so acutely. Rather, it will be to structure his inner life around these four areas – worship, study, solitude and service – as Jesus demonstrated so powerfully in his earthly life. As Matt looks at Jesus, he will gain the confidence that this is the best possible kind of life and that it really works. He will find himself profoundly challenged and greatly inspired.

And he will need to be. It seems so counter-intuitive to suggest that for Matt to find himself, he will need to place the weight of his very existence on God. It feels more like losing himself, and indeed in a way it is. He will need to give proper place to his mind, when it is his soul that is shrieking out to him that something is wrong. He will be asked to spend time alone, which is where he most does not want to be. And lastly, Jesus points him to a life of addressing the needs of others, when it is his own needs which are so pressing.

This might all seem strange to Matt, not to mention frightening. It can come across as surprisingly non-religious. But it is a copying of Jesus. It requires faith – we need to trust the Lord, in this as in everything else, that this truly is the way to life. And it requires more than good intentions. It requires action. And to that action we turn in the next two chapters.

4. Vision for life with God

Raj is in his late twenties. He is a software engineer and works in London. He loves his job and the excitement of being at the heart of one of the world's leading financial centres. His home is India and his family still live there. He has been in the UK for some years now, and has taken to Western culture like a duck to water. His job has given him lots of money, a great place to live, many friends, and access to a partying world of which he has taken full advantage.

Last spring his mother died unexpectedly. He could only take a week off work to go home for the funeral and to be with his family. The shock of his loss and the clash of cultures as he returned to rural India made him think carefully about his life and where he was going.

On his return, he found the relentless drive of work, London life, superficial friendships and short-term relationships based on sex curiously shallow. He found himself thinking about what kind of a person he was. He wondered about his mother – what would she think of him now? He thought of the slow pace but spiritual values of his upbringing.

He met a girl one weekend at a party, and found himself opening up to her about these deep and personal questions. She said that she was a Christian, and invited him on an Alpha course – an opportunity to explore the meaning of life and to see whether the Christian faith had anything to say. He liked this girl and agreed to go to the first evening of the course.

To his surprise, he loved it. He really liked the people, and the guy giving the talk seemed to be talking just to him. How did he know what Raj was thinking?

Over the next few weeks, he felt himself changing. He thought about things differently. He started to pray, well sort of – he did not really know what to call it, but he felt God was close to him. He was fascinated by Jesus – in fact he even prayed a prayer asking Jesus to come into his life. In all honesty, he did not feel any different, but he thought it was the right thing to do.

And then came the talk on how and why to read the Bible. The speaker was a young woman who was highly dynamic and great fun. He really liked her. She talked about having a relationship with God as she read the Bible. She used the image of walking in the woods and hearing bird song, and having your ears attuned to the beautiful sounds of the birds.[1] He had always loved birds – they reminded him of India. And the idea of a beautiful sound, which had always been there but for which he had never really listened before, totally gripped him.

That night he bought a Bible. He wanted to listen for the bird song. But it was a huge book. When he opened it at home, he flipped it open and read randomly. He put it down an hour later. He was disappointed and a bit confused. It didn't read like bird song at all.

I once helped on a Christian camp for eleven- to fourteen-year-old boys. There was a talk on reading the Bible. The speaker asked the boys to choose between the Bible and a million pounds. His point was that the Bible is 'more precious than gold, than much pure gold'.[2] Not surprisingly, the boys opted for the million pounds.

At the time, I was really on the boys' side of the fence. I was pretty new to being a Christian and, well, a million pounds was a million pounds. But the Bible's power and wisdom have grown in me, and now I think I really would take the Bible any day.

Raj's experience is very common. On the one hand, the Christian claim is that when we read the Bible, we hear God's voice. We really do hear the bird song. But on the other hand, the realities of handling a book of the Bible's length, complexity and cultural difference are very great.

Let's look at the place of the Bible in copying Jesus.

Jesus and the Bible

As we saw in the last chapter, Jesus modelled a life that is saturated in the Scriptures. His way of understanding the world came from the Bible. He understood his own identity and mission with reference to Scripture. And he heard his Father's voice as he read.

Take the time when Jesus is tempted in the wilderness by the devil. Here is high drama, with so much at stake. Jesus is physically weak, drained, alone and vulnerable. The devil comes to lure him away from the hard road of his mission to save the world. Jesus' response is to cite three passages from the Old Testament Scriptures. The first one is pertinent to our discussion: 'It is written: "People do not live on bread alone, but on every word that comes from the mouth of God."'[3] The devil is tempting him to satisfy his physical appetite – he is hungry – by turning stones into bread. Jesus responds by talking about the Bible. What is going on here?

A vision for life

Jesus found his vision for life in the Bible. The direction the Bible gave him was more important to him than his physical hunger, and more compelling than the 'sensible' but diabolical tempta- tion. He meets each of the three temptations in the same terse, non-negotiable manner: 'it is written'. The temptations differ – they concern his mission, his identity and his obedience to the Father's will. For each, the Bible supplies his response. The scriptural vision is greater than all other competing visions of life, and gives him the freedom to respond as God's Son.

Our situations will obviously be different, but we can adopt the way in which Jesus looked to the Bible of his day (the Old Testament Scriptures). There are many competing visions that bombard us every day. This is particularly true in the areas in which Jesus was tempted: what we are to do with our lives, our sense of who we are, and our relationship with God. Some of these visions are compelling. There are those which seem to have the authority of received wisdom, and to command universal acceptance. The visions of consumerism, materialism, hedonism and individualism seem self-evident to most in Western societies. But the Bible gives us a different vision for our lives and identities and relationship to God. Jesus' example encourages us to allow our deepest values and vision for life to be moulded by the Scripture. In the Bible, God himself gives us his vision for life.

It is as if we were going on a long walk. In the closing stages of the walk, we are told to orientate ourselves by looking to the church steeple on the far-distant horizon. We have been walking all day and the weather has not been brilliant. We are cold and hungry, and looking forward to getting back. The bad weather sometimes makes it difficult to see the church spire. We come across a road. Someone suggests that it would be far more sensible and much easier to take the road, rather than keep going towards the church, not least because we are now walking across quite difficult terrain. The person making the suggestion has no real knowledge of where the road leads, but because they speak with such conviction, many do follow them down on to the road. We determine though to keep following the church steeple. We are safely back after an hour's hard walking. The others get terribly lost and have to retrace their steps, before picking up the church trail again.

The road vision is deeply attractive, but not really based on truth or knowledge. The church vision gets us safely home.

Jesus signals an approach to the Bible which realigns the way we look at the world and think of ourselves and our lives. All our minds are stocked with visions of life, personality and reality that come from many different sources. We don't really think about most of them and accept prevailing wisdom without question. But Jesus lays before us the Bible as God's vision for life. The Bible helps us to understand God, his world, his purposes, ourselves and our lives.

We will often find this challenging. We may have to modify our own ideas and priorities in the light of God speaking to us through Scripture. We may have different ideas of who God is and how he acts. We may be challenged about our personal lives, or our attitude to money. We may find God's agenda for the world very different from our own or from what is regularly promulgated through the media, and we will be challenged about those whom society overlooks or despises. But it is God's vision. It is a splendid and glorious vision. And it does get us 'home'.

A power to live

Another feature of Jesus' response to the devil is the emphasis on being sustained by 'every word that comes from the mouth of God'. He says (quoting from the book of Deuteronomy in the Old Testament)[4] that it is as necessary for life as food. We cannot live purely on food; we need words from God too.

There is much in Scripture about the sheer power of God's words. Here are two supreme examples.

1. God makes the world by means of his words – famously, he speaks and it springs into being. 'And God said, "Let there be light," and there was light . . . '[5] The Psalms say, 'By the word of the LORD the heavens were made, their starry host by the breath of his mouth.'[6] The New Testament letter to the Hebrews talks about how Jesus is 'sustaining all things by his powerful word'.[7]

2. Jesus raises Lazarus from the dead. How does he do it? Does he lay hands on the corpse or stretch out his body over him, or breathe into his dead mouth? No. 'Jesus called in a loud voice, "Lazarus, come out!"' And we read, 'The dead man came out.'[8] It makes us think back to earlier in John's Gospel, when Jesus says, 'Very truly I tell you, a time is coming and has now come when the dead will hear the voice of the Son of God and those who hear will live.'[9]

This is awesome, almost unimaginable power. Things that previously did not exist come into being. The dead receive life again. This is of an order that is beyond the power of human beings. And this power is released through the *Word* of God.

In his encounter with the devil in the wilderness, and by quoting Deuteronomy 8:3, Jesus shows us that the Bible does not simply supply us with God's vision for life; it also carries some of God's own creative, life-giving power when we read it.

This explains the typical stance of God's people throughout the Bible. They listen. They hear and obey. Jesus gives us a model of discipleship that is based around listening. The disciple copying Jesus makes a point of carefully listening to God's word, with awe, humility and faith.

There is a marvellous prayer of the apostle Paul's, where he says, 'And we also thank God continually because, when you received the word of God, which you heard from us, you accepted it not as a human word, but as it actually is, the word of God, which is indeed at work in you who believe.'[10] That is the same model as that of Jesus. When we hear God's word, we believe that something happens. We receive it, not just as good advice or some spiritual insight, but as God himself speaking to us. And when that happens, his divine, creative, life-giving energy gets to work in our lives.

This could help Raj enormously. When he comes to the Bible, he is approaching God himself, a God who speaks. Raj will be looking for something big to happen – his whole way of looking at the world and of understanding himself will be shaped and moulded by this encounter – but he will also be looking for some way in which he can truly hear this word and give it maximum attention. This opens up for him some practical suggestions for reading the Bible.

Listening to the God who speaks

If Jesus models for us both a big-vision approach and an attitude of awed attentiveness, then this pushes us in two directions for our own Bible reading. The first is a way of taking in Scripture's big vistas and perspectives so that they can shape our vision of God and life. The second is a much more focused reading, listening closely to every divine breath.

Big vision, big stories

Sometimes it is worth going to see a film in the cinema, rather than waiting for it to come out on DVD. This is the case for films with magnificent scenery or dramatic special effects. *There Will Be Blood*, for example, had to be seen on the big screen in order to take in the sheer vastness of the landscape in which the characters were living and working.

Bible reading is a bit like that. It is a big book, and sooner or later we will need to read a lot of it. Much of the Bible contains accounts of people and stories. This is not to suggest that they are fictional, but rather that they operate in the same way as stories do – there are characters and events, and things happen. The accounts are intended to be read complete, as a whole, and it is good practice to do so.

The Bible has many types of literature contained within it. Most famously, there are the Gospels, the accounts of Jesus' life, teaching, death and resurrection. Then there are numerous letters, a majority from Paul to the churches that he had founded. But there is also poetry and history. There are riddles and prophecy, apocalyptic literature and romance, and other genres too. The Bible itself encourages us to read it in different ways, according to what type of literature it is.

To see the great vista, Raj could settle down of an evening, and give his Bible a really good read. The bird song may well not be immediately apparent, but it will probably come in unexpected ways. Much of Genesis and Exodus read well in that way. The so-called history books, such as Samuel, Kings and Chronicles, also work well like that. Raj could divide up the big prophets like Isaiah and Jeremiah into large chunks of twenty-or-so chapters and read them at one sitting.

The point of this kind of reading is to see the big vision. Raj's prayer is that he might think big and true. He should not be distracted by details or minor questions. He should read the story and let it work on him. He will be surprised, even shocked, by some things. He will find that some of what he reads raises huge questions for him. He will sense ambiguities, and shades of meaning that elude him. He will be moved to tears by some passages, stirred to anger and pity by others. And throughout it all, he will be interacting with God on a huge scale. This is how God has acted in relation to a people (first Israel, and then the church) over thousands of years. God has chosen to reveal himself through how he has lived with people. He has acted in power, in love, in judgment, and always in grace and wisdom. People have worshipped him, betrayed him, trusted him, let him down, behaved well and acted with appalling badness. What can Raj learn from this? What is God saying to him about who he is and how life can be lived?

And the greatest vista of all is the Bible picture that snaps into sharp focus with Jesus. Jesus is the centre, focus and climax of the whole Bible story. He said that the Scriptures testify about him,[11] and after his resurrection, on one memorable occasion, he spoke with two of his followers, 'And beginning with Moses and all the Prophets, he explained to them what was said in all the Scriptures concerning himself.'[12] Good Bible reading will take this as the key to the big story of the whole of Scripture, both Old and New Testaments. Jesus is where the story is going to, and part of the joy, excitement and wonder is seeing how we catch glimpses of this long before he is born. Jesus is prophesied. People seem to behave as he will behave. The structure of the world is made understandable to us in terms that only a divine sacrifice can explain. There are dreams and visions of a future that only a God on the earth can fulfil. And so the story continues.

Listening as if your life depended upon it

One of the jokes of the TV series 'Allo, 'Allo was the line, uttered in a parody of a French accent, 'Listen very carefully, I will say this only once.' For real spies, of course, information needed to be both communicated and received accurately, for lives depended upon it.

Jesus' second approach is one of total attention – an attitude of close listening. The sheer privilege of hearing the living God speak is almost overwhelming. The Bible has metaphors of Scripture being like gold and silver and precious stones, like water to the thirsty, food to the starving, life to the dying, healing to the sick, and light and direction to those who have lost their way in the dark. All these images show us the preciousness and value of the Word of God to us.

Some American soldiers were captured by the Japanese in the Second World War and imprisoned in one of the notorious labour camps. One man had a Bible with him, which he was able to hide from his captors. To keep it safe from discovery, and to enable the maximum number of men to read it, he tore it into separate portions, some as small as a single page. The pages were cherished and passed round all the men. These pages gave life and hope; they kept faith alive. Those captives read the words of God because their lives depended on them.

Raj will try to find a way of reading the Bible in more detail and with greater attentiveness. Many people find it helpful to have a structure to this, perhaps a daily routine. There are many publications around now which make this very easy and are a great help.

This is probably where the bird song will be loudest for Raj. He will find it best to stop and be quiet. This is not like flicking through the newspaper on the bus on the way to work. This is a special, holy time, when he is drawing close to listen carefully to God speaking to him. It is more like reading poetry than scanning a manual for a new gadget. He will want to pay attention to words, ideas and phrases that seem to leap out at him. He will treasure what he has heard, and keep mulling it over in his mind. He will pray about what he has heard, meditating on it, taking the full goodness into his system, and releasing the power of God's truth into his life.

Living the vision

Jesus shows us the fully human life. He models for us that this life is structured around worship, study, solitude and service. As we come to the first spiritual discipline of Bible reading, we see Jesus modelling all four aspects of this fully human life.

He worships. This is God's word. The heart of it is the living God speaking in love and truth to bring our minds and lives back into conformity with him and his ways. We worship God by paying him maximum, focused attention, honouring him as we listen to him.

The discipline will require our most precious resource: time. We shall want to make the most of this by applying our minds in study and finding solitude so we can give our full attention to God speaking to us.

And this focusing on the God who speaks will have an impact on us. We will find ourselves changing. Bible reading will lead to action. James writes, 'Do not merely listen to the word, and so deceive yourselves. Do what it says.'[13] We will act on what we hear. It will lead to service of God and others.

Bible reading is not an end in itself. The aim is not to acquire knowledge so that we can be champions at *Bible Trivial Pursuit*. The aim, as with all the spiritual disciplines, is to be with God, so that he can be glorified as we live out this fully human life that Jesus has won for us on the cross and has modelled for us by his earthly life.

A friend of mine once built a kit car. It was an absolute monster. It was huge, lurid, magnificent. It looked fast and ugly. My friend gave me the full guided tour. He told me about every part, and the history of its construction. He explained the intricacies of the engineering, the brilliance of the design. We gazed raptly at the colour and the shape. We looked at the seats, the dashboard, the multiple gears.

And then we got into it and he turned it on. I have never heard anything like it! It was the loudest engine in the world; it must have been. The whole thing shook. The earth seemed to move. Then he drove it. Out on to the little country lane, then round the town ring road, and on to the motorway. Then he really let it rip!

The car was fascinating and looked magnificent. But it was built to be driven and driven fast. It was for driving, not for being admired.

The Bible is endlessly fascinating. There will be no end to the books written on it. But it is meant for relationship with God. It is designed so we can hear the living God speak to us. He speaks Jesus to us, our Saviour and Lord. And he speaks of how to be truly and fully alive, how to be the people he made us to be, the people we long to be. The power of God's Spirit in the Word is such that this becomes possible. As we pay attention to the God who speaks in Scripture, we are remade after the likeness of Christ, the image of God.[14]

5. Prayer and life

Emma was really uncertain about praying. She was
slowly coming to Christian faith and beginning to attend
church. She loved the singing and the sense of the
presence of God with her. She loved the Bible, but
praying was something else.

For one thing, she thought it was false. She had grown
up being taken to church and 'suffering' in school
assemblies. The rote praying she found boring and
insincere. Now she was coming across people who
prayed out loud, without prayer books. She found it
unnerving. It made her think of cults and brainwashing.

And when she did try to pray on her own, she
sometimes found it unsettling. Unwanted feelings came
to the surface, bizarre memories and thoughts.
Sometimes she just had to stop it and carry on with her
day. Frankly, it made her nervous.

To be fully human, we pray. It is in praying that we grow into
our own truest selves. Jesus was the perfect, most authentic
human being who ever lived, and he was also the pre-eminent

man of prayer. We all pray in our individual ways, and we may well find that we pray differently at changing seasons of our lives. But however we do it, to be fully ourselves, we will want to learn to pray.

Jesus, the man of prayer

If the heart of discipleship is being like Jesus, we will want to look at how Jesus prayed so that we can copy him. This is precisely what his disciples did. We read in Luke's Gospel, 'One day Jesus was praying in a certain place. When he finished, one of his disciples said to him, "Lord, teach us to pray."'[1] In response, Jesus instructs them by giving them what we have come to call 'the Lord's Prayer'. There was something compelling and attractive in Jesus' praying. The disciples recognized in his prayers something crucial in his life, and they wanted to know how they could do it too.

The Lord's Prayer is reported to us by both Matthew and Luke in their Gospels. In Matthew, Jesus introduces the prayer by saying, 'This, then, is how you should pray . . . '[2] He offers the prayer in contrast to the showy, empty prayers of religious hypocrites. In Luke, he is responding to the disciples' request to learn how to pray. When we put both contexts and introductions together, we are being taught a pattern of prayer in the one (Matthew) and a form of prayer in the other (Luke). Straightaway, Jesus is teaching us two major lessons in prayer.

The pattern of prayer

There is a wrong way to pray (to show off, to impress God, to feel good about how spiritual we are) and there is a right way to pray. Jesus gives us the right way to pray in the Lord's Prayer. It translates to just fifty-two words in English:

Our Father in heaven,
hallowed be your name,
your kingdom come,
your will be done,
on earth as it is in heaven.
Give us today our daily bread.
Forgive us our debts,
as we also have forgiven our debtors.
And lead us not into temptation,
but deliver us from the evil one.[3]

It is short and simple. It is the prayer we teach our children, and it may well be the prayer we eventually pray on our deathbeds.

We can reflect on these words and divide them into two basic categories. The first five lines are about God. The second five are about us. Jesus gives us a model of prayer that is half-worship and half-intercession. We begin by focusing on God, and then we finish by asking this God to supply our needs in life. As we pray, we position our lives in relation to God – first in worship and then in intercession. We gladly acknowledge that he is God, as we praise him, and then we acknowledge that we are not God, as we pray from a point of utter dependence on him.

Jesus' pattern of prayer begins with the God-ness of God. He is 'in heaven', his name is to be honoured, he has a kingdom, his ways are pre-eminent and best for all on earth. This is consistent with the orientation of Jesus' own life, as we saw earlier: worship is foundational. We find our humanity in humble, trusting relationship with God, who is both our Father and our King.

The pattern prayer then moves on to praying for ourselves. We come to God in all of our humanness. There is no pseudo-piety here. We pray for our needs, both material (bread, debts) and spiritual (forgiveness, temptation, protection). This is dependence on God for life and breath and everything. Every time we pray the Lord's prayer, it is as if we come to God to be created all over again. In prayer, God makes us alive.

This model of prayer is like good conversation. When we meet up with someone, we first ask about them, and then (if they are interested) talk about ourselves. When we pray, we start with God and his concerns. We rejoice in our relationship to him as Father, we worship him as special beyond words, and we pray for him to change the world, for his glory and the world's good. The pattern tells us that this will account for about half of our prayers.

The second half is talking about us. The joy of prayer for the Christian is the certainty that, possibly unlike the person we have just met up with for conversation, God is definitely interested in us. It is almost as if he is more interested in us than we are in ourselves. There is nothing too practical, mundane or unspiritual for us to pray about. This pattern of prayer covers money, housing, diet, health, strength, relationships, emotions, person-alities, habits, life choices, protection. Jesus helps us to see ourselves as totally dependent on our Heavenly Father for everything. He is the source of all good gifts. In him we can find spiritual resources to live good lives. Without him, we are vulner-able and at the mercy of forces too great for us. With him, we can be fully alive, fully human and our truest selves. And we can be in relationship with him, and be agents for the coming of his kingdom on the earth.

So prayer is both more and less spiritual than we would imagine. Half of it is about God. Prayer is prayer when it engages with God and his kingdom. Jesus shows us a pattern of prayer that lifts our minds and spirits beyond the everyday. We are taken up with God and we pray for the world as he sees it.

But then we pray in a seemingly very non-spiritual manner about the everyday, details that we should imagine are too mundane to concern God. Christian prayer is unashamedly asking for things: 'give', 'forgive', 'lead us not', 'deliver'. It delights God when we acknowledge our dependence on him and our trust in him so that he can supply the answers to our requests.

The form of words in prayer

In Luke, when the disciples ask Jesus to teach them how to pray, he replies, 'When you pray, say . . . '[4] The message seems to me to be, 'Use these words.' We are moving now from a pattern (you should include these things, these areas) to what we actually say. Prayer usually involves words, and the words themselves matter.

I think the practice of the majority of the Christian church down the ages and across the world is right. Praying the actual words of the Lord's Prayer is a keystone to learning to pray. These are the words that Jesus gave us. We want to learn how to pray? Well, here it is – pray this.

This raises wider and more practical questions for me. Is this the only way to pray? How else did Jesus pray? And there's the whole concern that praying set prayers seems somehow inauthentic, not personal, and so somehow not true. Let's look at three ways in which Jesus prayed.

More about Jesus the man of prayer

Personal prayer

We see Jesus on many occasions clearly praying from the depths of his being, in response to some particular need or situation. Jesus' prayers are intimately connected with life. He prays at the major points of his life. He prays at the crises and at the points of decision. He prays at the points of anguish, bereavement and pain. He prays for direction, he prays about his friendships and his life's work.

And when he prays, he does so both more and less than we should imagine. He prays whole nights, he prays when others are sleeping, he deprives himself of sleep and company. When he needs to pray, he really prays. But he also prays short prayers along the way, outbursts of praise and thanksgiving, poignant in their directness, and cries of pain.

So personal prayer is both extraordinary and everyday. It is both extreme and casual.

I find all this immensely encouraging and stirring. Prayer is as natural as breathing in the sense that it becomes part of our lives, both in the large and small events. Jesus shows us a companionable form of prayer, teaching us to recognize and be grateful for the presence of God throughout the day. We turn our hearts in praise for a glorious morning, a child that makes us laugh, a colleague's friendship, or we cry out under our breath for help, wisdom, courage at points of challenge.

And then there will be times when we will really set ourselves to pray. I do not think that Jesus made a regular practice of praying all night. He did it, not out of routine, but out of need. There are times in our lives when we really must grab hold of God, or things will slip away from us. Maybe there will be extended times when we cry out to God. It may not be terribly coherent, but we will be praying from the heart. This will be from the depths: 'O God, help me. Help me deal with the loneliness, the fears that come from nowhere, the secret shame. O God, heal me, hold me, save me. Dear Lord, show me, guide me, protect me. Save me from myself. Have mercy on me.'

Perhaps this will be the lonely struggle into the night. Perhaps it will be a long walk on a Saturday morning. Maybe even a conversation with a good friend, consciously in the presence of God.

There are times in our lives when there just is not the time or energy to pray in a formal or structured way. If work starts early, and evenings are taken up with marking or preparation; if the children are young and never stop, and we have just not got any spare emotional capacity; if we are not well or facing depression: in all these and many other situations, the idea of sitting down and praying for any length of time is not realistic. And we can compound matters by feeling guilty for what were unreal expectations in the first place.

At these times, we learn to pray on the wing. There may be a bus journey or time in the car. There may be a bonus ten minutes as we walk to the post office or pop out to buy sandwiches at lunchtime, or that time immediately after the children are in bed. Learn to be with God then, to bring ourselves with or without words, and lift our lives, concerns and loved ones to him.

I am sure we see Jesus doing this. Bear in mind that there were times when he was too busy even to eat, or when the pressure of the crowds was near to overwhelming him. We read illuminating sentences at these points: 'Very early in the morning, while it was still dark, Jesus got up, left the house and went off to a solitary place, where he prayed . . .'[5] and 'Jesus, knowing that they intended to come and make him king by force, withdrew again to a mountain by himself.'[6] Here is the element of solitude in Jesus' life which we saw earlier. Even though we will have individual personalities, and some of us are drained by solitude and need company to energize us, Jesus encourages us to make solitude a part of our lives. He seems to make a point of being alone at times of maximum stress and pressure, as in the two examples above. The supreme example of course is the Garden of Gethsemane, when Jesus prayed alone for three hours before his arrest and crucifixion. The value we each attach to being on our own will vary with our personalities. But when this is time with God, it enables us to draw strength from him, to regain faith, wisdom and perspective, to process our lives with the help of the Holy Spirit. For many people, consciously held periods of silence greatly enhance and deepen their prayers – a time for meditating on a Bible verse or holding up a person to God in prayer, or being open to the Holy Spirit's still, small voice.

Some find it helpful to make times of solitude a regular pattern, and actually book in time away. There are now many places which are set up for this, and some offer help with praying. But it is not necessary to go to a specialist retreat centre. We can create our own space: an evening walk, a weekend with friends with space built in, even a chair which everyone knows is your quiet chair. The iPod can be great for this too: why not listen to some worship music, or to the Bible being read, or to a sermon, and take God into everything else you are doing that day?

Structured prayer

So we have Jesus praying naturally and spontaneously. This seems real and true to us in our age, which is so wary of the inauthentic or the false. But Jesus gives us a form of words to pray. He would also have used formal liturgies and written prayers. We read of him going to Nazareth synagogue on the Sabbath day 'as was his custom'.[7] The early church combined worship in homes with regular attendance at the temple services, something which they would have learned from Jesus. These services, in both synagogue and temple, would have been highly liturgical, with set prayers, blessings, actions and responses. Jesus would also have been used to a regular saying and singing of the Psalms, the Bible's song book, a practice which carried over into the early and later church, and which persists to this day. Jesus gives us an approach to prayer that is counter-cultural to many in the West. It seems there is value in set forms and patterns of prayer, something that can really help us to realize our full humanity.

Tom Wright[8] helpfully explains:

There is nothing wrong, nothing sub-Christian, nothing to do with 'works-righteousness', about using words, set forms, prayers and sequences of prayers written by other people in other centuries. Indeed the idea that I must always find my own words, that I must generate my own devotion from scratch every morning, that unless I think of new words I must be spiritually lazy or deficient – that has the all-too-familiar sign of human pride, of 'doing it my way', of, yes, works-righteousness. Good liturgy can be, should be, a sign and means of grace, an occasion of humility (accepting that someone else has said, better than I can, what I deeply want to express) and gratitude.[9]

It occurs to me that this is what all churches right across the board do when it comes to singing songs and hymns. Why are we happy to do this when it comes to singing, but not to non-musical praying?

So maybe we can find comfort and inspiration from some of the ancient prayers of the church. *Common Worship: Daily Prayer*[10] is the Church of England's daily prayer book, and there are many others. This framework, and the sense of praying with others, can give a real sense of strength, and may well help us with the underlying issues of our lives. C. S. Lewis used to say that he never prayed the liturgy but rather prayed 'through' the liturgy. The ancient words are like a window, for looking *through*, rather than looking *at*. So we could find ourselves in God's presence, with the gift of words to say, space in our hearts, and inner landscapes for the Spirit of God to strengthen and heal, at precisely those points which so rarely see the light of day, but which are increasingly making their unwelcome presence felt.

There is something here too about routine. Historically, many of the services of set prayers were written to be prayed and sung at different times of day. The idea was that each day would be somehow boundaried and filled with prayer and Bible reading. This would have been the practice of Jesus and the first Christians too – they followed the set Jewish hours of prayer.

Much of modern life dislikes routine, and for many of us our personalities and approaches to life share this contemporary antipathy. Again Jesus is offering us a way of life where ancient wisdom challenges modern perceptions. The spontaneous is not necessarily the best, the most authentic or the most satisfying. Jesus encourages us to pray regularly, to build routine into our lives, as well as spontaneity.

This gives us structure in our lives. I can think of some people who only pray when the mood takes them. They justify this on the basis that to do otherwise would be hypocrisy and would not be in tune with their personalities. In truth, if they could but see it, they are in desperate need of structure and routine. Their championing of the spontaneous and the natural can be hiding inner chaos and disorder. To learn to pray regularly would be a momentous blessing for them.

I remember, for a year, praying my way through the Lord's Prayer each morning. I had a dog, Basil. He and I would go for a walk early each morning round Hyde Park in London. I would pray each petition of the Lord's Prayer and then let the Spirit take me into other areas of prayer that flowed from it. Often I would not get further than a particular phrase. For several days I would be anchored in a specific part of the prayer. It was a very rich experience and shaped the whole year. That was the year that Catherine and I got engaged, when I started a new job that was to prove immensely significant for me, and when painful issues from my past were dealt with and put to bed. And I brought it all to the Lord daily in prayer.

Finding a routine is crucial in the spiritual disciplines, so that we can genuinely resource the fully human Jesus life. There will be days when we just do not feel like praying, yet these may well be the days when we actually need to pray more, not less. We may be facing pressures which pull our minds away from God, yet it's precisely on those days that we need God to be strengthening and guiding us more than ever. We may be facing challenges at work, in our relationships, with our health, in our concern for our loved ones. Our lives may be getting out of kilter, distorted by the demands life is putting on us. If we depend on our own volition as our inspiration, we will probably not pray. What routine does is that it brings us to God, whether we feel like it or not. It also establishes a pattern of relating which can deepen and change over time, but which is also a constant – a kind of personal faithfulness. And such is the power of routines that it is actually involving our bodies as well as our minds and spirits.

Of course, routines can kill. If they become dull and lifeless and empty of meaning, then it is better not to do anything at all. And different personalities react to routine in different ways – some of us are creatures of habit to our fingertips and others need variety just as we need fresh air each day. But it is instructive to me that Jesus, the perfect human being and our model and inspiration, used routine. We would be wise to practise rhythm and routine ourselves.

Prayer in the Spirit
God lives in the Christian by his Holy Spirit, and Jesus shows us to the full what this means. He was conceived by the Holy Spirit, became strong in the Spirit as he grew as a child, was anointed by the Spirit to preach good news to the poor, was led by the Spirit, healed through the Spirit, and spoke words that were both Spirit and truth. He also prayed in the Spirit. 'At that time Jesus, full of joy through the Holy Spirit, said, "I praise you, Father, Lord of heaven and earth."'[11] He taught us that we need the Holy Spirit to pray,[12] a teaching which is repeated and developed throughout the rest of the New Testament.[13] If we are to pray like Jesus and emulate his perfect humanity, then we will need to pray in the Spirit.

At one level, all prayer is Holy Spirit prayer – we cannot pray without the Spirit. But at another level, it is apparently possible to pray without the Spirit.[14] Since the Holy Spirit is fully divine, as much a person of the Holy Trinity as the Father and the Son, what Jesus and the New Testament are holding out to us is a model of prayer which sees God and us praying together. When we pray in the Spirit, God is praying in and through us.[15] Our prayers are inspired by him, and we join with him in prayer. What an extraordinary thought!

Paul's prayer life has lessons for us at this point. He describes his own prayers in 1 Corinthians 14:14–16. He writes of praying and singing with both his understanding and his spirit. I think the point of the contrast is that, under the influence of the Holy Spirit, Paul's spirit can sometimes think and pray in ways he does not fully understand. At times Paul does not make it clear if he is talking about the 'Spirit' of God living in him, or his own 'spirit'.[16] This interpretation is confirmed by the way that Paul rounds off the argument by saying, 'Otherwise when you are praising God in the Spirit, how can the others . . . say "Amen" to your thanksgiving, since they do not know what you are saying?'[17] So what we see of Paul's prayer life is a mixture of singing and praying, and a mixture of praying with his mind and praying with the Holy Spirit, in ways which the mind cannot fully grasp.

Jesus speaks of knowing the things of heaven, of speaking God's words because God has given him the Spirit without limit. The Spirit has come down and remains on him. He is the man of the Spirit. It is in the Spirit that he communes with his Father, receives direction and guidance, and sees what his Father is doing. Can we think of it any other way, when we consider his anguished prayers in the Garden of Gethsemane, when his 'soul is over-whelmed with sorrow to the point of death',[18] and 'his sweat was like drops of blood falling to the ground'?[19] The writer of the letter to the Hebrews puts it like this: 'He offered up prayers and petitions with fervent cries and tears to the one who could save him from death.'[20] I am sure some of these prayers were 'wordless groans', which is how Paul describes praying in the Spirit.[21]

Even if all Christian prayer is Holy Spirit prayer, there seem to be times and a type of prayer which can be more fully designated 'prayer in the Spirit' than others. It is prayer that goes beyond words and beyond understanding. It is in those times that God himself prays through us, melding our hearts with his own. He searches our spirits with his Spirit, shows us his will and desires, and heals our own hearts and hurts. Sometimes this prayer finds verbal expression in groans or other languages and tongues. Sometimes it is accompanied, as with Jesus, with great anguish or with joy. This is prayer of great privilege and power.

Our own prayers should have space for this kind of Holy Spirit praying. It is a recognition that prayer is more than words, and that human beings are more than just mind. It is prayer when the whole of us meets the whole of God, and we are filled with his loving, glorious presence. It requires the attention of the human spirit and a radical openness to the love and ways of God. It is the recognition that in prayer, as in all of life, it is God who takes the initiative, and it is our privilege to respond and follow him.

Being filled with spiritual wisdom

In one of his great, rolling prayers, Paul prays: 'We continually ask God to fill you with the knowledge of his will through all the wisdom and understanding that the Spirit gives, so that you may live a life worthy of the Lord and please him in every way.'[22]

The main thrust of Paul's prayer is that the Colossian Christians should carry out lives worthy of the Lord, lives that please him. He wants them to be human beings fully alive, with the whole of their lives (not just the spiritual bits) glorifying God. How do they get there? It is as God gives them spiritual wisdom and understanding. These are words from the Old Testament – they imply lives that are lived well, based on an experience of the living God, his word and presence. This can only come, Paul says, through the Spirit – that is, the Holy Spirit.

The poet W. H. Auden said, 'One of the troubles of our time is that we are all, I think, precocious as personalities and backward as characters.'[23] The fully human life is one in which we grow to know who we most truly are and can be in Christ, and are filled with the ability to become that person. We do not just become good Christians, but good human beings. Prayer is where that process happens. We become human as we pray. When we pray, God makes us alive.

The distinctions which I drew between those three aspects of Jesus' praying (personal, structured and Holy Spirit prayer) are very artificial ones. Good liturgical prayer can be both personal and Spirit-filled, for instance. But I think it is true to say that to live like Jesus we need to learn to pray like Jesus, and to pray like Jesus will mean learning to involve the whole of our lives within the ambit of the Father's kingdom, praying regularly and steadily with words sometimes not our own, and to pray from a heart full of the Holy Spirit. We will each find different ways of doing these things according to our circumstances and temperaments, but the road to the fully human life will include all three approaches.

6. When life is hard

George and Ethel are in their eighties and live in a little house in one of the new developments in a university town. They are two of the most serene, kind and obviously saintly people that I have ever known.

George is a retired GP. He came to Christ as a student, and after completing his medical training in one of the London hospitals, he got married, and then he and his new wife went overseas as medical missionaries to an African country. They were enormously happy there and were widely loved and respected. Their two children were born in Africa.

Tragically, George's wife died in Africa. After a spell at home, George and the children decided to return. He spent the next twenty years there. He met Ethel and they fell in love and got married.

The African country where George and Ethel were working suffered a military coup. Showing great personal courage and incurring enormous risk, George and Ethel sheltered the outgoing leader in their home to enable him to leave the country. Today, they still have a gift from him in their home. Under the new regime, however, it became impossible for them and the children to continue to live and work there, so they returned home.

George took up his GP work again in Berkshire, England. He and Ethel joined their local village church, where they were extremely loyal, even though some might have said that not much was going on. George and Ethel approached the vicar and, with his blessing, set up a youth club. They continued to lead it for the next five years, when it had grown to over fifty young people. They always attributed its success to the power of prayer and the amazing God to whom they prayed.

Just after George retired as a GP, his elder son died of cancer, while still a young man. He was a radiant Christian and, while strength permitted, he toured the country telling people about how the Lord was sustaining him through his cancer, and how he was facing death with courage and confidence in the face of what would happen after death.

Today, old age is difficult for Ethel. She has painful arthritis in both hands and she broke her hip in a fall. Getting around is becoming an increasing problem.

Both George and Ethel exude peace. They welcome young people, and their home remains a place where many come for prayer and peace. Their hospitality is legendary, even though it is increasingly difficult for them. They never miss the church prayer meetings, and to listen to them pray is somehow to be in the presence of holiness. Their faces shine, their faith is an encouragement to all, their love a comfort and strength to all they meet.

Holding faith and life together

If the aim of discipleship is human flourishing, then what about those parts of life which are tragic and marked by suffering? What is the place of struggle for the Christian? How is following Jesus to be real, and not a retreat into a kind of spiritual fantasy world of make-believe?

It is a caricature, of course, but it is sometimes said that if we come to Jesus, then all will be well. Partly this has to do with our culture which finds sickness, hospitals, sadness, death and bereavement notoriously difficult to cope with, and either ignores it all or puts it on *Oprah*. But it is also to do with a defective theology, which effectively isolates faith from the real world and casts God in a sort of magician's role: his task is to wave his magic wand and put everything right. If things go wrong or stay wrong, then God has not performed his tricks. His very *raison d'être* is called into being, and we are left either to limp along in our increasingly troubled and unconvinced faith, or, sooner or later, to abandon faith and the church, feeling disillusioned and bitter.[1]

So what should we expect? Will a fully human life be free from suffering? And if it isn't, then how can we handle it?

The sufferings of the people of God

Let us start by looking once again at the life of Jesus. Bear in mind that he is the perfect image of God – this is the ideal human life, the ultimate model for us to emulate as we were created to do, as we discover and live out our own truest selves. And here is the shock: the ultimate destination of Jesus' life was the cross. He lived to die. He presents to us an ultimate human life which takes love and self-sacrifice to the harsh reality of death. This is very different from our usual conceptions of self-fulfilment and self-discovery. It seems that, for God, self-preservation and self-fulfilment are in different categories. A fully human life will not be one which defines itself by comfort and the avoidance of suffering. It is the opposite: the fully human, Jesus-life to which we aspire as his followers will actually, in some sense, embrace suffering and bear it for the sake of others.

So we see Jesus engaging with suffering and sorrow. He brings in the kingdom of God which reverses the effects of human alienation from God and one another. But he does so ultimately on the cross by taking it upon – and even into – himself. And he offers his followers the same paradigm: 'Whoever wants to be my disciple must deny themselves and take up their cross and follow me.'[2] In taking on human flesh, he takes on all the weaknesses flesh is heir to, becoming vulnerable to sickness, sorrow and death. He plunges himself into the milieu of betrayal, violence, misunderstanding and rejection. The Gospel accounts of his death show us a man at the extremes of physical, relational, emotional and spiritual agony. We are in the world of political violence, torture, abuse, powerlessness, the destruction of a human being by the powers that be, because he has become both inconvenient and expendable. The darkness of those last three hours on Calvary show us humanity seemingly abandoned by God, crying out in the darkness. Here is a life which has ended in failure, where all that he has built on has proved to be illusory and powerless in the face of real power. Violence wins. Secularism, military might, manipulation and corruption, the kingdoms of this world win. The devil wins – it is his hour. Gethsemane was for real, the stakes were massive, darkness triumphs. It is only later, in the light of the resurrection, that we can see the hidden power of God's love at work.

Once we start to look for it, we find suffering and darkness everywhere in the biblical narrative. The Bible starts in the book of Genesis by giving us a portrait of a family that is highly dysfunctional, marked by sibling rivalries, terrible parenting, drunkenness, incest, even murder within the family. Exodus shows us a picture of God's people in slavery and appalling suffering. The Psalms give us songs of terrible despair and depression, as well as songs of praise and joy. The New Testament gives us a picture of a fledgling church that advances as much through suffering and martyrdom as it does through miracle and triumph. The last book of the Bible, Revelation, interprets the world for us through an apocalyptic lens: the picture is of persecution of the church, human wickedness running amok, and terrifying visions of plagues and fire.

So being a follower of Jesus is not about being immune to suffering. Christian faith is not a magic wand to make all nasty things go away. In fact, it may even be the opposite: we are more, not less, likely to encounter suffering. So George and Ethel were not surprised at the terrible sufferings that they went through. They could have thought, 'Here we are, serving the Lord at considerable personal cost – surely the least he can do is bless us by protecting us from these personal tragedies.' But they did not. Somehow, they found a way of embracing tragedy and suffering. Without wanting to sound trite or blasé, this extraordinary grace in their lives was revealed in their depth, holiness and even joy. I do not know if they would agree with this, but to the outsider, it seemed that their lives were actually so filled with God *because* of their sufferings, not in spite of them.

We are called to the cross-shaped life

Broadly speaking, we can say that there are two forms of suffering: one that comes as a result of our choices, and the other that comes to us and our loved ones seemingly from outside. Jesus speaks of both.

Here he is talking to his disciples and some who are intrigued by him: 'The hour has come for the Son of Man to be glorified. Very truly I tell you, unless a grain of wheat falls to the ground and dies, it remains only a single seed. But if it dies, it produces many seeds. Those who love their life will lose it, while those who hate their life in this world will keep it for eternal life.

Whoever serves me must follow me; and where I am, my servant also will be. My Father will honour the one who serves me.'[3]

Jesus begins by talking about the cross, and how he, 'the Son of Man', is to be glorified. He describes it in picture language as a grain of wheat which has to fall into the ground before it can produce a huge harvest. The cross is death, and no mistake, but it is a kind of dying that will produce life on a huge scale. And he and the Father will be glorified.

But then he extends this principle of life through death to all who would follow him. It is at the level of a general principle: 'Those who love their life will lose it, while those who hate their life in this world will keep it for eternal life.' We all know that hoarding a thing, or isolating a life, actually causes it to turn bad and sour. Spiritually, it is the way of death, not of life and flourishing. Jesus then applies this to his followers: 'Whoever serves me must follow me.' The disciple is committed to walking the same path as the Master. Christians follow Christ and copy his life, a life that was all about the cross.

And his life is about life through the cross: 'where I am, my servant also will be. My Father will honour the one who serves me.' Jesus is headed for glory through the cross; he is returning to his Father. This is the path he holds out to his followers, together with the favour and honour of his Father in heaven.

This opens out wide vistas for us. The Jesus-life is all about life after all. Everything we have been thinking about is validated here. It is the kind of life which is true life, life that is stronger than death itself, and which has the power to spill over to others too. What Jesus says here is that this kind of life is actually resurrection life, and resurrection only follows death. It is life through the cross. We are called to the cross-shaped life.

What does this mean? It means that just as Jesus lived a life of obedience to the Father that was for the good of others and the world, even at the cost of his own needs and desires, so must we. Just as Jesus lived a life serving other people, healing the sick, proclaiming the kingdom in word and deed, confronting injustice, giving priority to the poor, reaching out to the margin-alized, bringing the good news of God's love and life to all, so must we. And the template of this cross-shaped life can be laid over the major events of our lives and the tiniest details. Jesus gave his life on the cross in a huge and public display of self-sacrifice. He also stopped to pay attention to children, to notice the lame and the blind, to embrace the outcasts, to wash the feet of his friends and followers, to pour out his heart in prayer.

So we are not called to ease and comfort in copying Jesus. How could we be? Christian discipleship is not a more spiritual version of the advertiser's dream – a perfect life of health, wealth, beauty, satisfying material and sexual relationships, all lived in a dream home, miles from unpleasantness. It is a life in which overall we put ourselves last. It is a life that is lived only through the conviction that the cross is the way to life.

There are versions of Christianity around that belie this. 'Come to Jesus and you will have wealth and health. Treat church as if it was a consumer choice, and when you don't like the music any more or you run into trouble or boredom, then move on. It's all about *me*, my desires and fulfilment.'

It is hard to see how such a life could truly be called a copying of Jesus.

There are some qualifiers, but not many. We are not called to a masochist lifestyle. It is not wrong to enjoy life and all its blessings. Wealth, health, lovely homes and fine things are not wrong. We should care properly for ourselves and our loved ones. Self-indulgence is not evil. But the main point still stands, that the overall tenor of our lives should be marked, even defined, by the cross.

Why would we be willing for such a thing? This is almost a deliberate embracing of suffering; it is not natural. We do it out of obedience to Christ and for the Father's favour. We do it because we believe this is how Jesus lived, and we will find the fullness of our humanity and our own truest selves in following him. And we do it in the conviction that life, in this world and the next, will follow from it, both for ourselves and for others.

I met an advertising agent who followed Jesus by leaving a well-paid job and plush London lifestyle, and joining a medical charity working in some of the most dangerous places in the world. I came across a man whose response to Jesus' love was to throw himself into putting together a furniture store where the poor could receive donated, good-quality furniture. I think of countless young people who take time off work, or use a precious Saturday, to redecorate homes for those in need.[4] Then there is the aspiring politician who founds a project using drama to help ex-offenders get back on their feet. Or the lady who cares for her elderly mother, day in, day out, for many years. Or the young people who give up two evenings a week to work with other local young people. Or those who give money generously and sacrificially to finance evangelistic and mission work. Or the countless people whose every action and encounter with others determinedly puts the other first, and does so with warmth and a whole heart.

Such a life is a tough calling, and it will come to us all in different ways. It can feel agonizing. It should do, because it is the way of the cross. But it is the way to life, the fully human life.

We are called to Jesus in the pain of the world

We are called to be with Jesus right in the centre of a world of pain and despair.

Later on in John's Gospel, Jesus says to his disciples, 'I have told you these things, so that in me you may have peace. In this world you will have trouble. But take heart! I have overcome the world.'[5]

He is telling them about his own impending death, and foreseeing their consequent confusion and despair. He tells them that the resurrection will bring them joy. Now that they know these things, they can find peace and even a sense of being invulnerable in the middle of the troubles that they will face.

Jesus talks about 'this world', which implies the existence of another. This is both the new heaven and the new earth that is to come, but he also calls it the world that we can experience now, 'in me'. The outer world is a world of trouble, especially for the followers of Jesus. The word translated 'trouble' more literally implies pressure or stress. 'You will be pressurized and stressed in this world,' Jesus is teaching. 'You need to know this, so that when it happens, you won't be thrown, but instead have peace.'

The world as it currently stands is profoundly disordered. It is still unspeakably beautiful, but it is also marred by being out of joint. Death rules and defines existence. Wickedness and evil seem to triumph. Selfishness and violence dominate societies everywhere. The planet is under environmental threat. Natural disasters cause untold havoc and suffering. Disease and sickness, personal anguish, insecurity, fear, financial disaster – the list could go on.

The call to copy Jesus means experiencing precisely this world, but to do so from the dual perspective of being 'in him' and from the world that is to come. This world is fraught with decay and death. But Jesus has, through his cross and resurrection, changed and healed all that. We will see the fullness of that at the end of time, but we can experience that coming reality, in part, right in the midst of our own present experiences of loss, sickness and suffering. 'Take heart! I have overcome the world.'

The fully human life is found even in terrible darkness by discovering Jesus in the middle of our sufferings. In him we find a peace about the present and a confidence about the ultimate future. It requires that we 'take heart'. Sometimes faith is much more like courage than anything else. Grief and suffering can assault us. It takes bravery to hold to faith at such times. We are following Jesus down the path of embracing the full fallenness of this world as he goes unflinchingly to the cross. And as we trust in him and keep following him, we believe that we will find the resurrection life to come, and some of that will spill over into the pressures and stresses of our present experience.

When things go wrong and bad things happen, we are often quick to turn on God in anger, with a sense of betrayal and of being let down by him. This is understandable, and there is much scriptural warrant for such an approach. Both the Psalms and the book of Job show us individuals engaged in angry and accusatory dialogue with God over unjust suffering. Jesus' last cry from the cross, 'My God, my God, why have you forsaken me?',[6] can be taken at one level as a cry of accusation and sense of betrayal.

But longer-term healing usually comes when we move on from there to sensing how God can work, even through these terrible events, for good. We find Jesus at the heart of this damaged and wounded world, crying from the cross. We are with him there, and he with us. He bears pain as well as sin.[7] And we find a way with Jesus to look to his overcoming of the world, and to his recreation and healing of the creation: 'But take heart! I have overcome the world.'

I saw this in the examples of my breakfasting friends, James and Simon. Both have lost their mothers recently. Simon's mother was ill for a very long time. He visited her faithfully and regularly throughout the time of her decline. He speaks fondly, especially about spending New Year's day with her. By this stage, she wasn't able to communicate in any usual way. He would sit with her and talk to her, holding her, uncertain as to how much she understood, but occasionally, unmistakably communicating through a reciprocated squeeze of the hand. They might listen to the radio or perhaps share a beer in the grounds of the home, watching the sun go down together. Often they would just sit in companionable silence. Simon would say that their relation-ship had always been loving, but not always easy. During the long hours and months of her decline, Simon would sit and pray, sometimes aloud, but usually just silently. By the time she died, their relationship was healed, and they were both able to pass on in peace, Simon to the next phase of his life, his mother to glory.

James's mother died of cancer last year. She was the chair of the local cancer hospice and it was to the hospice she went to die. Her decline was a series of downward steps, and her death was quick when it came. James and all the family were able to be with her in her last days. They were all able to say their farewells and to tell her that they loved her. She died at peace and full of faith, and confident of what lay ahead for her. James was able to put into practice the lesson he is always encouraging Simon and me to learn at our breakfasts: what is God doing here? For James, in a wonderfully natural way, his mother's passing was full of God, of his love and presence, guiding his mother to her heavenly home, and him and his family through the sometimes raw emotions of loss and grief.

I so admire my friends (and am so grateful to them for letting me quote their examples here). This is authentic Christian discipleship, which can search for, and find, the hand of God in suffering. Both men were not small in stature before, but they are now even more impressive. They have not become all solemn and pompous (we laugh far too much at our breakfasts for that!), but they do have a seriousness, a maturity about them. They have weathered tough times with the help of God's Spirit, and they are all the more impressive, more human because of it.

By contrast, I am sure we all know people for whom tragedy has been a blight on their lives, and the further tragedy of bitterness has been added. Where grief has not been resolved, where anger or fear persists, where trust with God or others has not been rebuilt, it is like a wound that has covered over but underneath it is still unhealed and prone to repeated infection. We all know how that happens, because it happens in our lives too. We need Jesus to bring us healing and freedom, and to lead us into the future he has for us.

Fullness of joy

George and Ethel learned these lessons well over the course of their lifetimes. Through, perhaps even because of, their personal tragedies, they came to a place of extraordinary spiritual reality. This was not anything mystical, but it was through praying and reading the Bible, and faithfully and humbly serving God every day of their lives for over eighty years. They copied Jesus, developing the fully human life, both through suffering and joy. They were not afraid of death, either for themselves or for their loved ones. They could face anything with calmness and steadiness and courage. They lived well all their lives through thick and thin, and it gave them the confidence, even the joy, to face the future with trust and serenity. I have changed their names, but their story is true. I knew them in the 1980s and now they have gone on to glory. I know they died in all the faith and comfort of Jesus, and now they are enjoying fullness of joy in his immediate presence, knowing God even as he has always fully known them.

Do you want to live like that? I certainly do. It comes about through authentic discipleship, through following Jesus in this cross-shaped life. It comes from a lifetime of bringing our real lives into the loving presence of God. Whatever happens, however terrible it might be, with the daily grace of God, we can know his love, sympathy and transforming hope. It is the truly human life, being totally free through the love of God, because not even death and tragedy can take from us our true humanity and our ultimate destiny.

7. Why go to church?

Tom and Karina went along to church one Easter Day. They did not really know why. They were expecting their first baby and it just seemed the right thing to do. To their surprise, they really enjoyed it. The reality of the spiritual nature of the experience touched them, as did the genuine warmth of the people they met there. Karina had gone to church as a child, and she was agreeably surprised at how different it felt now.

So they went again. They met more people and became good friends with one couple. When their baby was born, they had a very special baptism service for him. It was a happy day, with their families and friends from all over the world. The church seemed such a hospitable and right place for such an occasion.

So now they are thinking, 'What next?' They like the church. They feel something spiritual stirring within them, a growing belief in God and an experience of his presence with them. But the baby has been baptized, so there is not so much of a reason for going. And now life is crazily busy, with a young child, work stepping up, moving to another flat.

How does church fit in? How does it fit in with their burgeoning beliefs? And, more to the point, with their hectic lifestyle?

I can imagine that, in certain quarters, the very idea that church can be a good place would raise a derisory snort. Common perceptions, and alas sometimes common experiences, of the church are not favourable. Churches are perceived to be 'institutions' or 'organizations', not warm, interdependent communities or factories of human flourishing. They are thought to be about one man (and in the perceptions it is usually a man) at the front, who is authoritarian and out of touch, or weak and flaccid. Church is thought to be like a hobby for some, a means of escaping from the pressures of real life. It can even be dangerous – a place where abuse occurs, and out-moded, repressive ideas are imposed on increasingly unthinking people, usually the vulnerable. All in all, it is not usually a happy picture, far removed from the idea that it is in churches that God's great work of setting people free to be themselves takes place.

Yet local churches are the epicentre of God's transforming work on this earth. And in terms of experience, I know scores, maybe even hundreds, of people, who in churches have discovered loving, supporting communities in and through which they have found the reality of God.

Authentic discipleship, human flourishing, cannot be separated from the church. Getting involved, and thoroughly so, will be at the heart of how God will shape and develop us as his people. This does not necessarily mean being committed to the institu-tion or even the programmes, but it does mean committing ourselves to the public worship of the church and to the people there. Unless we give time and energy to these things, we will find that the transforming impact we long for in our lives will not materialize.

Jesus and church

'Jesus came to found the kingdom of God, and what we got was the church.' According to the gag, Jesus seemingly did not found a church when he was on the earth. Rather he inaugurated the kingdom of God in an explosion of teaching and healing, embracing of the poor and the outcasts, and culminating in his confrontation with the powers that be, which led to his death on the cross. He only spoke about the church twice,[1] and made no provision for the conduct of worship or the hierarchy of church leadership. So, if we are taking Jesus as our model of the fully human life, where can church fit in?

It is not really possible to separate Jesus from the church, once we see church, not as an organization, but as a community of those who are following him. The great missionary theologian, Lesslie Newbigin, puts it well: 'It is surely a fact of inexhaustible significance that what our Lord left behind him was not a book, nor a creed, nor a system of thought, nor a rule of life, but a visible community.'[2] And again: 'Jesus . . . did not write a book but formed a community.'[3] To see Jesus gathering people around him is a rich way into understanding church as integral to discipleship.

Matthew's Gospel is particularly concerned for Jesus' followers to see themselves as the people of God. The followers of Jesus are not to see themselves as individuals in relationship to Jesus, but rather as the continuation and development of God's ancient people, Israel. Israel in the Old Testament is to be the model of how the church is to be in the New. So Matthew begins his Gospel with that long list of Old Testament characters from Abraham to Jesus. Why? He is placing Jesus firmly in the context of the major events of the story of the people of Israel in the

Old Testament. He sees Old Testament history as moving from Abraham to David to the exile in Babylon to 'Jesus who is called the Messiah'.[4] He is showing us Jesus as the fulfilment of the major sweeps of God's dealings with his people. He is helping Jews see Jesus as the Messiah, but he is also helping all of us take Old Testament models as our means of understanding Jesus and what he came to do. One of the fundamental Old Testament categories is the awareness of being a people, not just a collection of individuals following God. So Jesus, in fulfilling the Old Testament design, places himself at the head and at the centre of a group who would understand themselves in relation, not just to him, but also to each other.[5]

The people of the Messiah

Matthew presents us with Jesus as the Messiah. The word 'Christ' is the Greek word for the Hebrew 'Messiah', which means 'the anointed one'. The Messiah is God's appointed King of his people and the one through whom God is to exercise his loving and just rule over all the earth. Jesus is that Messiah. And we are the Messiah's people. If we think of it in Greek terms, to be Christians is to be people of the Christ.

This means that to be the church is fundamentally to be the community that is at the disposal of the Christ. We exist because of him. We are for the praise of his glory. We are shaped and formed by his words and by his Spirit. We want to be like him as individuals. And as the communal body of the church, we want to be doing the same things that he did, and having the same agenda and impact that he had.

The strange absence of Jesus
But he is not here. Jesus died, was buried, was raised from the dead and then ascended into heaven. He is present through his Holy Spirit still, but we do not have that same immediate presence

as in the days when he was physically on the earth. So, strangely, the church is defined by the *absence* of Jesus. We love and worship Jesus, and try to live like him and with him, through the help of the Spirit. But the fundamental stance of the church is that we are *looking for* Jesus. And because he has promised that one day he shall return in power and very great glory, we are looking *forward* in time to that great and wonderful day.

There is a lot of material on this subject in Matthew's Gospel. Jesus tells the parable of the wedding banquet,[6] in which people are invited to the wedding of his son, but many refuse to come. The climax of the story is the king's arrival at the wedding. There are three consecutive parables in chapter 25 about living life now in the expectation of a future event: the arrival of a bridegroom for his wedding, a master coming to review the investments of three of his servants, and a surprising evaluation of the way in which the people of God have treated one another. In each case, the application is to be looking forward to the return of Jesus, and to be living now in preparation for that event.

So the Messiah's people live in a strange kind of tension. We are led by a Messiah who is not here. Our core business is to be available to him, so we are constantly looking to him, deliberately putting him at the centre of all we do. And yet the way we do this is by looking forward in time, anticipating his return to take his rightful and central place, not just in the church, but in the whole world.

For Tom and Karina, it will help to see church not in terms of what happens in a building on a Sunday, but as a group of people to whom they belong. They have become attracted to Jesus Christ and have a sense that he is calling them. His call is to belong to this group of people, and to go on a kind of pilgrimage through life with them. They need to challenge the prevailing notion within themselves that their individual life is how God will become real to them. God says that it is through this family of the church that he will shape their lives most profoundly, and cause them to have the effect on the world that they are longing to see.

I was very moved by a visit from a man who had just been evicted from his home and was in danger of being lost into a street lifestyle. What had happened was that three men from the church had come and found him, booked a hostel for him to sleep in that night, and fixed him up with an estate agent who found him a new (and better) flat the next day. I knew of none of this. The man just said to me, 'This is why I come to this church.' Church is not just individuals: it is organic; there is a shared life. God works in love through us all.

Lower expectations of church

What does this mean practically? How will this affect our attitudes and expectations of church?

Can I suggest that it means that church gatherings are where we renew our vision of Jesus, and are strengthened in our hope in him? We come to church to see Jesus, but also to wait for him.

I hope this does not sound too strange, but maybe something we have to do is to lower our expectations of church. Sometimes we are given the impression that churches are pretty much the kingdom of God on earth: constant miracles of healing, the days of the apostles once again, continuous revival. Or maybe it is couched in terms of the perfect community: loving, supportive relationships, with never a cross word. Perfect, error-free teaching. All prevailing prayer and evangelism. World-changing church!

Now, great and wonderful things do happen in churches, but if church is built round the absence of Jesus, our hope is in him and his return, not in the church working without him (albeit in the power of the Spirit). It is as Jesus returns that we shall see the kingdom fully come. It is only then that we will see the fulfilment of all God's promises to heal the earth. It is not right to expect everything to be put right before that day.

Sometimes I meet people who are very disillusioned by their experience of church. Sometimes it is just too drab: the music uninspiring, the preaching dreary, the praying vapid. Or else they find themselves disappointed in the welcome they did or did not receive. Or they are hurt by someone, or feel that they let themselves down. Let's remind ourselves that church will always be imperfect. Let's try not to be disillusioned. And we do this by recognizing that Jesus is not here. We put our hope first of all in him, and then only secondarily in his church.

Higher expectations of Jesus

But if we are to lower our expectations of church, church will help us raise our expectations of Jesus. Church is central in showing the vision and keeping it bright and clear. Theologian Geoffrey Wainwright says that it is through the worship of the church that 'a vision of reality which helps decisively in the interpretation of life and the world' is transmitted. He says that 'worship is the place in which the vision comes to a sharp focus'.[7] Richard Foster makes this great and very challenging statement: 'If worship does not change us, it has not been worship.'[8] Both men are highlighting the transforming nature of this vision: setting mind and heart on the future, not on this world, keeping our identity Christian. Our singing, praying, Bible reading and preaching, celebration of the sacraments, exercise of the gifts of the Spirit – all that we do in church – keeps the vision of Jesus and our identity in him bright and clear.

One Sunday, after an evening service, a friend of mine brought a friend of her mother's to meet me. It was the first time this woman had been to church. She was in floods of tears. This did not encourage me! I had hoped that the service would have been an encouragement, and yet this lady was clearly feeling worse after church than before. My friend introduced her to me, and said, 'She wants you to explain the doctrine of the Trinity to her!'

I looked at the woman and heard myself say, 'No. I think you want to give your heart to Jesus Christ, don't you?'

'O yes, yes, I do,' replied the lady. I don't know which of us –

me, my friend, or her mother's friend – was the more astonished by this exchange!

As we talked, it became clearer what had happened. It was during the singing that this lady had become emotional. She said it was not the music; it was the love. She had felt utterly over-whelmed by love. The songs were about Jesus and what it meant to be in relationship with him. And the woman had felt the reality of that love and wanted to experience this Jesus for herself. It was truly wonderful.

I wish I could say that that sort of thing happens every Sunday! This is far from the case, but that experience has always encour-aged me. This is what church does. We look at Jesus. We sharpen our vision of him, and increase our hope and longing for his return and the coming of his kingdom.

We need church to keep our hope in Jesus bright and clear. It is all too easy to adjust our views and expectations of Jesus to those of the prevailing culture around us. We begin to take our models of what it is to be truly human from other sources. We slip back into apathy or despair about the state of the world and its future. Church is the place where we have our vision sharpened that Jesus is our hope – for ourselves and our lives, and for the world and its future. The Messiah's people need to be looking for the Messiah, for his future and his kingdom.

The people of the Messiah's mission

Another of Matthew's great themes is that Jesus sends us on mission. Right at the end of the Gospel, Jesus sends the disciples away: 'Go and make disciples of all nations, baptizing them in the name of the Father and of the Son and of the Holy Spirit, and teaching them to obey everything I have commanded you. And surely I am with you always, to the very end of the age.'[9] Since the calling of the first disciples, Jesus has put mission at the heart of what it means to follow him – 'Come, follow me . . .

and I will send you out to fish for people,' he said.[10] He has already sent the Twelve out to proclaim the message of the kingdom.[11] Now, after his resurrection, he sends them again, this time to all nations. And this time, he promises them his presence.

We come to go

Here's another strange tension: when we approach church, our mindset is that we *come* in order to *go*. We are a missionary people, so our general direction is always out. We come together in order that we may better go out to love and change the world. Jesus has commissioned us to bring healing for the sick, freedom from evil for the oppressed, a community for the lost, life for the dead, as we all come together into this new community that he is building.

This means that church needs to be at one and the same time a welcoming community for all, geared towards the care and nurture of all people, but also a community of which the fundamental character is missionary.

It is human nature to create a community that is self-serving. It is usually beyond us to live in social groupings that are open to others and their needs, especially when these are in conflict with our own. This is why our churches can very quickly take on the character of what sociologists call bounded sets, where membership is clearly defined, even when no words are used. We need to resist the centripetal forces that drive our churches inwards. Jesus sends us *out* with the good news of his kingdom.

I attended a mid-week group in our church the other day. We were talking about what church is for. As we went round the room, there were some really good answers. 'To study the Bible.' 'To grow in faith.' 'To support one another.' 'To pray for one another.' Just then someone read out a text from a friend who was on a work visit to the slums of Mumbai. He had spent the last three days on a mud floor the size of a bathroom with twelve people. 'Life is rubbish,' was the terse conclusion. It felt like the voice of God to me. Church was not primarily about us being cosy and comfortable in an inward-looking little group. It was about the needs and anguish of the world. We needed to be ready to go. Our coming together was only to prepare us to go out again to love and serve the Lord in the world.

The benefits of mission

It is often when we engage in mission that we come to sense the presence of Jesus with us most clearly. This is of course in line with his promise to his followers in Matthew 28: 'I am with you always.' This has certainly been my experience. The times I have grown most in my faith have been those occasions when I have had the strongest sense of being sent out by Jesus. It has often felt a bit of a daring step! Giving a talk to some teenagers about Jesus. Going overseas to do some development work in Peru. Visiting an old lady near home. Helping at a homeless shelter. Leading at a Christian camp for boys for the first time. Painting the flat of a disadvantaged family near our church. Taking part in an Alpha course. Each time I felt the strong sense beforehand that I really did not want to do this, and there were very many excellent reasons why I should be doing something really important (like watching TV or paying bills or watching paint dry). These have not always been easy experiences, but I am so glad I did each one of them. I got a sense of what Jesus meant when he said, 'I am with you always.'

The Christian life is a life more of verbs than of nouns. It is a 'doing' faith. We are responding to Jesus, being sent out by him.

We do mission as part of what it means to be his people. We come together, we have the same great vision of Jesus and his kingdom. Then he sends us out. Often it is as individuals to live our lives for him, but there are times too when we do mission with others – in groups, as friends, even as whole churches. These are often very precious times.

When a new vicar came to a church that had seen hard times, he and the congregation began to face outwards and be more involved in the life of the local community around the church building. One local man said to the vicar, 'I have lived here for thirteen years, and I never knew there was a church nearby. Now, the blinking church is everywhere!' He was impressed. And the church was experiencing a renewal of its life together.

Church helps us to grow as human beings

If being like Jesus is what it is to be fully human, then to engage as his people in the kinds of activities in which he engaged is part and parcel of discovering our humanity. In a sense, Jesus sends us out to discover ourselves, as much as to do good. It is in the discovery that we are part of a missionary church that we grow as people as well as Christians. Often we get much more out of these ventures of faith than we manage to give. It is part of God's wonderful design of how human beings work and grow.

Bill is in his second year as a student. I saw him only last night as he was leading a student group in our church. It was wonderful to witness. He was warm and confident, brilliant at drawing people in, a great encourager. He led superbly. I thought back to a discussion I had had with him six months before, when he was all but crippled by self-doubt, lacking confidence in either himself or God. What had made the difference? It was being sent by Jesus, stepping out as part of the Messiah's missionary people.

Polly now lives in Italy where she has become a writer. When I first knew her, she was a trainee solicitor, working as an anonymous and not particularly happy part of one of the huge firms in the City of London. What had given her the courage to discover herself, turn her back on a life that was not really her, and to launch out into the uncertain waters of living abroad and earning her living as a writer? It was her regular life in the church, being stretched and encouraged by her friends, and taking on missionary challenges as and when they arose. I remember her going out to Kyrgyzstan to speak at a missionaries' retreat there. What a challenge! And how she grew through it as a person.

Following on from the home group meeting at which the text from the slums of Mumbai came in, we have all agreed to break into smaller groups of three or four and to explore our local area, praying as we go, and looking for ways to be involved. We have already made startling discoveries, and the whole dynamic of the group has changed. We are animated in a way that we were not before. We have a new sense of purpose, more energy, and we are actually closer to one another than before. We just feel more alive.

Tom and Karina can be involved in how God wants to change the world. By getting to know the local Christians in their church, they can forge good friendships and grow in their faith. But they can also work together within the church to bring God's love to those around them. It is through joining in with the church's worship and mission that they will most fully find themselves.

To the ends of the earth and to the end of time

Life is often full and busy. The pattern of our society is that weekends are precious refuelling times, either for hobbies or socializing or 'down time'. Church, by contrast, seems alien, operating on somewhat out-of-date social principles. Why would we rearrange the way we order our lives and our calendars? It takes an enormous effort of energy, both physical and emotional.

We can only do it on the basis of a wider reconfiguring of our lives. John Wimber, the founder and leader of the Vineyard Churches in the last years of the last century, used to say that three conversions are necessary: to Christ, to his cause and to his church. It is as fundamental a part of Christian faith to see our place in the church as it is to see our place in Christ and how we might live our lives in his service.

God's church
The church is the people of the Messiah. The Greek word for church is *ecclesia*, from which we get the word 'ecclesiastical'.

It has its root in the Hebrew phrase for assembly or gathering. Both the Hebrew and the Greek mean 'called out'. On their own, the words are largely synonymous with our own word 'meeting'. It is just a gathering of people. It says nothing about the purpose of the meeting. What makes the idea of church different is the One *by whom* we are called out. The phrase can only be fully understood within the wider understanding that the church is the gathering of people who have been called out *by God*. The people of Israel were called from out of all the nations to be the people of God in the Old Testament. Jesus is the fulfilment of that calling: called out in order to fulfil God's purpose for the healing and salvation of the entire world. As the Messiah, Jesus fulfils and performs that calling. As the church, we find our identity and our own calling within the identity and calling of Jesus the Messiah. In his name, we carry out the great mission of the kingdom of God to the world. And in so doing, we increasingly find our own fullest identities and humanity.

That means that church is right at the centre of what it means to be a Christian. It also means that church, crazy as it may seem, is the path by which we will discover most truly who we are and what we are meant to be and do with our lives.

I am a lifelong Arsenal supporter. One of my favourite fantasies is of being at a home game in the Emirates Stadium. The match is an exciting one and things are going well. Suddenly a man appears at my elbow. It is Arsene Wenger, at time of writing the Arsenal team manager. 'John,' he says quietly, 'our centre forward is getting a bit tired now, and I think I need to take him off for a rest. I want you to go down to the dressing room and get changed into the Arsenal kit. Then, I want you to come out on to the field and take his place.' And in my dream, that is what happens. I come on and play for Arsenal. Needless to say, it is all stunningly triumphant!

The difference between being a spectator and a player is enormous. And to be asked personally by one of the top managers in the world to play for one of the best teams in the world would be a great privilege.

When it comes to the church, God is inviting us to be on his team. He asks us to work with him in his church to bring his renewal and healing to the world. And the work is crucial and wonderful.

God's mission

Lesslie Newbigin describes the church as hastening to the ends of the earth and to the end of time. We are the Messiah's people, and his mission is to the ends of the earth, and he will be with us until the end of time, when he shall return again with very great power and glory.

An old boss of mine, the minister of a church in central London where many rich and powerful people live, once went to a drinks party. He was in a smart suit and tie, and not wearing his clerical collar. He got talking to a man who asked him what he did. 'Oh,' said my boss Charles, 'I work for one of the largest global operations in the world. We have millions of workers, outlets in every country in the world, a turnover of millions each year, work with the richest and poorest in every society in the world, and we are the world leader in our mission.' 'Ah,' said his companion. 'Which bank is that?' Charles smiled and told his new friend that he worked for the church.

Our local church is part of God's ancient plan to reach out to his world in healing and love. Churches are outposts of the kingdom of God. Churches are the most visionary places in the world – they have a global mission and one that is committed to bringing a universal future of blessing, salvation and joy. It is our privilege to meet with our fellow Christians to worship our God, Father, Son and Holy Spirit, and to be envisioned again by his greatness so that we can carry the good news of his kingdom to the ends of the earth and to the end of time.

A good deal of highly creative thinking is going on at the moment about the shape and future of how churches should operate. It is exciting to be around at a time when there is a resurgence of confidence and vision. Church is not just a date in our calendars, nor is it an organization set within an understanding of society which is rapidly fading from our cultural experience. The church is Jesus reaching out to a world that he loves. Church is dynamic and creative, animated by the Spirit of Jesus, praying and working for the fulfilment of the kingdom of God all around the world.

Our prime vision is Jesus himself. We look *to* him in church, Sunday by Sunday, and we look *for* him as we look forward down the, as yet, unknown paths of history's future. We need church to keep our vision of the vastness of Jesus bright and clear. And church needs us to fulfil the mission that Jesus has for the world. It will take our very best, our highest, our full potential, energy and love. And as we engage with Jesus and one another in his missionary church, we shall truly discover who we are and be shaped into the truest humanity.

8. Learning to love

This is a letter written by a lady in our congregation, which I find very moving and which I reproduce here with her permission. To understand it fully, you need to know that she is a lone parent. Her name is Susannah, and her delightful daughter is called Dana.

When joining the church, I felt for the first time that I wasn't being judged as a single parent. Nobody cared where I came from or who I was or what I had done (good thing too!) – I felt welcomed and cared for. My tiny little family became part of a huge, warm, loving family: God's family. It was this that drew me back week after week. I had felt myself to be judged by a variety of people previously, and had lost all sense of myself and my worth in society. Church life took me away from my own unsociable, morose, introspective company and into the friendly company of others, which benefited Dana most of all. Confident, safe and happy, I have found her the best family of all . . . but then again, I think she found it for me, and thus I found salvation!

Who are you?

I remember wandering round some bookshops in the week between Christmas and New Year. The displays were all about the 'New Year, New You'. The titles were similar to 'How to change your life in seven days' (there was one on how to change your life in forty-eight hours!), 'Destructive emotions – how to handle them', 'Hot sex – how to have it', and innumerable weight-loss books.

Our sense of our own identity is so crucial. How do we think of ourselves? I once watched some five- and six-year-olds taking a school assembly in which they spoke and sang in at least three different languages. I was quite impressed by this. I went up to one of the boys afterwards and said, 'You're brilliant!' He did not bat an eyelid as he replied, 'I know!' Now there is a strong sense of identity!

However, there are other more self-destructive voices, aren't there?

- Low self-image is rife in our society, even when it is clearly distorted. Sometimes this can be really horrible: 'Others are clearly right to treat me badly,' 'No-one loves me,' 'I hate myself,' 'I loathe my body.'
- Sometimes we define ourselves by our more destructive emotions: 'I am an angry person. I wish I wasn't, but I can't help it. That's just who I am.' Sometimes this is said defiantly, as if no further explanation or justification is necessary for some unacceptable behaviour. Other times it is said wistfully, with deep regret, with a kind of fatalistic resignation.
- At times we define ourselves in relation to some event in our past: 'I have been powerless since the divorce,' or 'I became a different person after the car crash.'
- There are times when we define ourselves by reference to someone else, or by membership of a group of other people: 'I am Tony's wife,' or 'I am my mother's son,' or

'I am just a working-class lad,' or, 'Our sort simply do not do things/think/act in that way.'

Identity and community

Part of what I find so moving about Susannah's story is that she felt more herself and more alive because of church. She thought of herself as morose and isolated, and she felt that she was judged by others. To come to church was to find herself loved and accepted in the wider family of the church.

Paul writes in his letter to the Colossians, 'Here there is no Gentile or Jew, circumcised or uncircumcised, barbarian, Scythian, slave or free, but Christ is all, and is in all.'[1] He is setting down all the major divisions in the way people thought of themselves and others in the ancient world, and then saying that in the church all these could be put aside. Instead of defining themselves in those old worldly ways, they could now relate to one another through Jesus.

It is in church that we find our identity in Christ. We relate to Jesus, taking him as our Saviour and our model. As we do this, we find that we are discovering our deepest and truest selves. Then, as we relate to others in the church, we find that true self strengthened and growing. We recognize Jesus in others and, in seeing him, draw closer to him ourselves. Tom Wright draws out some of the implications of this.

Wherever one looks, one sees Christ. When an elderly person is ignored, Christ is ignored; where a lively teenager is snubbed, he is snubbed; where a poor or coloured person (or, for that matter, a rich or white one) is treated with contempt, the reproach falls on him. There must therefore be mutual welcome and respect within the people of God. Nobody must allow prejudices from their pre-Christian days to distort the new humanity which God has created in and through the New Man.[2]

Jesus is drawing together a people to carry his kingdom to the ends of the earth. Churches are incubators of this kingdom. For all their frequent failures, they are the future because they are where Jesus is at work, recreating the human race. We were not originally created to be isolated individuals, but to be in relationship. That pattern of the original creation is repeated in the new creation. We are not being renewed in Jesus to be on our own, but to be part of the new humanity that is the church in Jesus Christ.

That is why Jesus can speak of his followers as being brothers and sisters.[3] The expectation is that we have a relationship with one another in him. He refers to us as his family; at one point, he points to his disciples and says, 'Here are my mother and my brothers. For whoever does the will of my Father in heaven is my brother and sister and mother.'[4] To belong to Jesus is to belong to one another as his followers.

An inclusive community

One of the most immediately striking features of the way Jesus dealt with people was the radically inclusive approach he took. It was so marked that it offended the religious stuffed-shirts of his day: 'The Pharisees and the teachers of the law muttered, "This man welcomes sinners, and eats with them."'[5] And again, 'If this man were a prophet, he would know who is touching him and what kind of woman she is – that she is a sinner.'[6] They called him 'a friend of . . . sinners'.[7] He was constantly associating with people whom others considered beyond the pale: sinful women, foreigners, children, drunkards, collaborators with the Roman occupying force, violent revolutionaries, the chronically and contagiously sick. One of his most frequently repeated actions was to eat with people like this, usually accepting hospitality at their hands. He acted out friendship and association with people on their terms. He treated them as fully equal to himself in social dignity and accorded them the same, or even greater, respect than he gave to the people of power and social prestige.

And he stressed this hospitality to others among his followers. Children especially were to be welcomed, and if anyone caused one of the little ones to stumble, they were to be subject to the severest penalties.[8] And if anyone was to wander off from the loving embrace of this community, then no lengths were too great to be taken to find and restore them.[9]

Church then is a place of radical welcome. No-one is to be excluded, however much they may be despised or derided in wider society. A mark of church then should be diversity. No single culture should have sway. No class or background should dominate another. No educational, ethnic or economic grouping has dominance. We are welcomed by Jesus into his family, and we welcome one another.

It pleases me enormously that, by the grace of God, our little church in the centre of London, on one random Sunday morning, boasted twenty-two nationalities. And again, giving glory to God, it is a sign of the reality of Jesus among us that in the last six years, we have had murderers, drug addicts and dealers, adulterers, alcoholics, street people, thieves and freshly released prisoners all worshipping with us. This is the sort of thing that happens when Jesus is in the midst of his people.

I remember going to church in Peru one Sunday. I knew precious little of the language and none of the songs. The liturgy and practice of the church were all foreign to me. But I experienced an amazing sense of fellowship in that church in the middle of nowhere in South America. The devotion of these people to Jesus was almost tangible – and I felt utterly at home.

So, when you and I meet in church, I am not John the minister, and you are not Simon the doctor, Anne the teacher, Bill the road sweeper, Terri from Australia, Douglas the Scot, Danny the local lad, Ben from Jamaica, Stevie the alcoholic or James from Eton – we are people who meet in Christ. Jesus is the one who defines us and who is our common factor. He is the foundation and bedrock, the lubricant and glue, of our community.

If the church can be pictured as a bicycle wheel and Jesus is the hub, then the closer we are to Jesus, the closer we are to one another.

The challenge of church

All of this is of course a double-edged sword.

Church is enormously encouraging. All are welcome. None are disbarred or black-balled. Every person is precious, and to be valued and treated with respect.

But church is also enormously challenging. Jesus expects to have a community of his followers. We are committed to one another as if we were family. And that includes people whom we would not necessarily have chosen as our friends.

This means that commitment to church is really commitment to people for Jesus' sake. If we are not in meaningful relationship with people in the church, then we are not in meaningful relationship with Jesus. We need to find a way of building relationship, of establishing community, if we are to see Jesus' vision of church fulfilled in our lives.

As I've mentioned, at our church we have mid-week groups. It takes time to get to the point of sharing at this level, but I have been deeply moved by countless stories of how love and friendship, prayer and the power of the Holy Spirit in these groups have brought individuals, couples and groups so much joy. The group of young men who pray together about their struggles to be sexually pure, the singles who uphold one another in their struggles, the bereaved man who is cared for by his friends in the group, the woman who is helped to come to terms with her griefs and fears, the many who find friends amid the loneliness of London, the groups who start going on holidays together, and those who are not Christians but come for the friendship and the acceptance.

This is church. It is about being human beings, about discovering and enjoying being ourselves – in community. I remember discovering Christian friendship at university, and the liberating, healing effect it had on me as a nineteen-year-old. It was not that I had never had friends before, and good friends at that; it was that I had never known friendships like this, where I had been able to bring myself into the orbit of love, acceptance and challenge. It is not uncommon on Alpha or similar courses like Christianity Explored for people to talk about the excitement of making new friends, and discovering Jesus in and through those friendships.

This is profoundly scary for most twenty-first-century Western people, for whom privacy, individualism and self-reliance are the pillars of our social creed. And it involves a complete rethink for many of us of what church is all about. It is certainly way beyond an hour on a Sunday morning! The church is God's community, where people are healed, and find themselves and find Jesus, through interrelationship. Church involves meaningful relationship, communication and commitment.

A school of love

'I have come to believe,' writes David Clark, 'that without a strong sense of community human beings will wilt and begin to die. Community is the foundation of human society, the zenith of interdependence, the epitome of wholeness; in fact, the end of our journeying. . . . Without a continuing and enriching experience of community, as well as a vision of its glory to keep us moving forward, all of us eventually perish.'[10]

The Bible as a whole would agree with this view in principle. Over against our culture, which increasingly says that we find out who we are on our own (from Descartes' 'I think, therefore

I am' – one solitary man, thinking, to the solitary hero of countless movies) – the biblical view says that we discover who we are through relationship.

A fair amount of Jesus' teaching about church relates to conflict: when brothers and sisters fall out, when someone causes another to sin, when people are driven away by the words and actions of others.[11] A central line of our daily prayer is, 'Forgive us our sins as we forgive those who have sinned against us.' Any relating with others that is beyond the superficial will lead to hurt and vulnerability at some stage. Jesus' community is committed to going beyond the superficial. It is in the church that we learn with Jesus what it means to love and to forgive, to build community in the face of human dysfunction. We could call the church 'the school of love'.

Think for a moment about how in Jesus we see the perfect life of compassion, kindness, humility, gentleness and patience. Think of him bearing with the disciples, forgiving from the cross. Think of his perfect life of love. This is our aim – this is what we want to be like.

This is why the difficulty of relating to people we do not like is actually the curriculum in this school of becoming like Jesus. A large part of becoming more human, more our best and truest selves, is to learn to get on with and, eventually, to love those people who are different from us and who may, objectively, be unlovely and treat us badly. We learn to relate to one another in love in the church – that is partly what it is for.

I'm sometimes amazed at just how much sin and hurtfulness there is in the church. Barely a week goes by without some fresh outbreak of conflict. Then there is defensiveness, there are stand-offs, little explosions, hurtful e-mails. Sometimes people leave the church, feeling betrayed and let down. 'These Christians are just like everyone else, maybe even worse.' Some just have had enough – they've tried so hard with people who continue to let them down and throw their efforts at friendship back in their faces. Some find that they just cannot make the kind of friendships they are looking for in the church. There are some 'elephants' in the church, who go blithely around treading on everyone's toes, without even realizing it. Others are defensive and prickly, emanating an atmosphere of blame wherever they go. Sometimes church services become exercises in tactically avoiding certain people – only to have an excruciating and tense moment of unavoidable contact in the queue for the loo at the end of the service!

What are we to make of so much conflict, bad behaviour and bad blood, and all in this community which is supposed to be the arena for becoming more like Jesus?

But this is the whole point. This is the furnace in which we are being forced, often painfully and almost never easily, to learn to love. The conflict is the process by which we are growing into our new Jesus-like selves. Jesus loves everybody, and it is the inspiration of his love and forgiveness which motivates us and empowers us to do the same.[12]

Central to the school of love will be seeing others through the eyes of Christ. We need to unlearn any old categories we may have had for looking down on others, or of judging them by the colour of their skin, their accent, or a personality which rubs us up the wrong way.

C. S. Lewis, in the wonderfully satirical *The Screwtape Letters*, presents us with the correspondence from a senior devil (Screwtape) to a junior one (Wormwood), his nephew, where Wormwood is given the charge of working on a young man who has just become a Christian: 'I note with grave displeasure that your patient has just become a Christian.' Screwtape advises Wormwood on what to do.

One of our great allies at present is the Church itself. . . . When [the new Christian] gets to his pew and looks round him he sees just that section of his neighbours who he has hitherto avoided. You want to lean pretty heavily on those neighbours. Make his mind flit to and fro between an expression like 'the body of

Christ' and the actual faces in the next pew. . . . Provided that any of those neighbours sing out of tune, or have boots that squeak, or double chins, or odd clothes, the patient will quite easily believe that their religion must therefore be somehow ridiculous. . . . Work hard, then, on the disappointment or anticlimax which is certainly coming to the patient during his first weeks as a churchman.[13]

It's so true, isn't it? And Lewis is right to help us see beyond it to the smear campaign of the enemy. A friend of mine was nearly put off becoming a Christian because the person in front of him had BO. Mercifully, he was able to see beyond that.

And it is not that we reserve these attitudes of love solely for church. Our aim is to practise them until they become part of us. And we learn them in church – it is learned behaviour which will not come naturally to us. This is the church really working – we are being stretched, and learning to love and forgive. We are not learning social skills, or looking for such skills in one another; we are learning profound attitudes and acts of love.

Church as the new humanity

Church then is not so much services or activities, still less institutions or denominations. It is people – people who, through following Jesus, have come into relationship with one another. In some parts of our culture, the whole idea of church is becoming more and more suspect, or at least odd. We need to recapture the sweeping vision that Scripture gives us of the church. It is, in Christian author John Stott's memorable phrase, 'God's new society'.[14] If God's plan is to see the whole earth renewed through the rescue and (re)creation of men and women through Jesus Christ, then the place where this starts is the church.

We can expect to discover still more deeply what it is to be human in churches. This comes through committed relationships with others who are following Jesus too. Often this is not an easy process, but there is a lot of unlearning for us to do. Our characters need to grow much more into the likeness of Christ, and this is a lengthy process.

But if this results in us being closer to Christ, more like Christ, more truly ourselves, and more effective together in showing Christ to the world, then it is very well worth it.

9. Healing the creation

John has just started his first 'proper' job after university. The hours are long and it is a steep learning curve. In addition there is the daily commute: forty-five minutes each way on crammed trains. He is enjoying the work, but finding it demanding, and he spends much of his working life in a permanent state of paranoia – surely someone soon is going to find out that he knows absolutely nothing about what he is supposed to be doing.

He is sharing a house with three old university friends, and that is great, although they see surprisingly little of one another. And sharing a house is a good deal more demanding than friendship from a distance at college.

Church is OK, but it is not a patch, John thinks, on his university church. The worship is not brilliant, and the teaching is dull and inclined to the moralistic and platitudinous. The people are very mixed, and there are very few in John's position in life.

Over the next year, John finds that his faith seems to lose the old fire and vitality that it had at university. He faithfully attends services on Sunday and actually goes to

> a mid-week Bible study fairly regularly too. But he is
> having to face the fact that in his faith, as in the rest of
> his life, he is just tired and feels weak.
>   What is he to do?

Here is the flip side of John's dilemma. It is taken from a summary
of a parable told by Kierkegaard:

> Søren Kierkegaard, the famous Danish Christian philosopher, grew
> up in the countryside surrounded by farms that reared geese (among
> other animals). Each spring he would watch as a new gaggle of
> goslings was hatched and began to be fattened for the table. Over the
> course of their short lives these geese would gorge themselves at
> constantly refilled troughs of grain until they were so fat they could
> hardly walk. He imagined that they believed their lives to be perfect,
> as every need they had was catered for in abundance.
>   When autumn came, the truth became apparent. The wild
> geese that had spent the warm summer months in Denmark
> would gather in preparation for their southerly migration. As
> they assembled to fly south they would circle in the skies above
> the farms, calling out to any stragglers to join in their flight.
> At this point the farmed geese would lift their heads from their
> feeding troughs and look into the skies, heeding the call of their
> wild cousins. For the first time in their lives they would become
> animated, running as best they could around their enclosures and
> attempting to fly. Of course, their glutinous diet and life of luxury
> meant that they were far too fat to get airborne – but still they
> would try. And then, as quickly as the commotion had started,
> the wild geese would fly off and the fattened farm geese would
> watch them briefly before returning to their grain to continue
> eating their way to their deaths.[1]

John's predicament arose because he was a farm goose and had
to learn to fly as a wild goose. He had been fed and pampered

in his Christian sub-culture for so long that the real world, and serving Jesus in the real world, left him feeling ill-equipped and tired. He was trying to flap his little wings, but getting airborne was an erratic and tiring process.

I can speak with authority about John because he was me when I left university and moved to London. My friends were fantastic, and so was the local church that I attended. The challenges I was facing up to lay within me.

These last two chapters are about flying. Geese are made to fly. Christians are made for bringing in God's kingdom on earth. Discipleship is not for thinking about in a darkened room, it is for living. All that we have reflected on in terms of the spiritual resourcing of the fully human life (both on our own and in the church) is with the aim of fuelling a life that is to be lived to please God, and which joins with him in his plans for the world. It is the culmination of being truly alive and truly ourselves.

There is work to be done

After his crucifixion and resurrection, Jesus appears once more to his disciples. This is what happens: 'Jesus said, "Peace be with you! As the Father has sent me, I am sending you." And with that he breathed on them and said, "Receive the Holy Spirit. If you forgive the sins of anyone, their sins are forgiven; if you do not forgive them, they are not forgiven."'[2]

Jesus greets them, commissions them and empowers them. They have work to do. The model is that of Jesus: 'As the Father has sent me, I am sending you.'

A huge change of gear is taking place here. The shaping of their lives to that of Jesus is now to be continued without his physical presence with them. They are to take his message – forgiveness on the basis of his death on the cross[3] – and they are to be filled with his own breath, the Holy Spirit. Here is the ultimate goal of discipleship: to be shaped by Jesus' message and mission, and to be filled with his own life. The disciples are now in a position, in a sense, to be Jesus for the sake of the world.

This feels to me like a culmination of our central theme: that the Jesus-follower copies Jesus. It is as if the materials for the new car are laid over the blueprint, and by some act of alchemy spring to life. The apostles have spent three years living closely with Jesus, listening to his teaching and observing how he lived his life. Now they are to take on that life themselves. This time the Jesus-life is empowered, not by his example and physical presence, but through his agenda and the indwelling Holy Spirit.

The Olympic Games in Beijing in China saw one or two unfortunate relay races, when the baton was spectacularly dropped. There is no way back when that happens, and the teams that dropped their batons were nowhere to be seen when it came to the medals.

This passage is like Jesus passing the baton to the apostles and, consequently, to us, his followers, down the centuries. There is something of the flavour of coming of age. All parents are ultimately trying to work themselves out of a job: their goal is the independence of their children, equipping them to live life without support. Just so here where Jesus is thrusting the disciples out into the world to continue the work that he has started.

It is hard to overestimate the challenge this must have been to the disciples. The baton had been successfully passed to them. What if they were to drop it? Theodore Roosevelt once said:

> It is not the critic who counts, not the man who points out how the strong man stumbled, or where the doer of deeds could have done better. The credit belongs to the man who is actually in the arena, whose face is marred by dust and sweat and blood, who strives valiantly, who errs and comes short again and again, who

knows the great enthusiasms, the great devotions, and spends himself in a worthy cause, who at best knows achievement and who at worst if he fails at least fails while daring greatly so that his place shall never be with those cold and timid souls who know neither victory nor defeat.[4]

I think there come certain watershed moments in our lives. Faith moves from something private and essentially interior to something public. It is acted on. In the terms we are considering here, the baton gets passed, the child comes of age.

It is no coincidence that the context here is mission. Jesus sends them. Our word 'mission' comes from the Latin word for 'send'. He 'missions' the disciples, and they come of age. The challenge to us and our maturity is the challenge of being sent by Jesus.

Many fears can arise at this point: 'I am not worthy – I would just let the side down,' or 'I am not ready yet,' or 'I'd like to, but I'm just too busy,' or 'I didn't sign up for this – this is fanaticism, sect-like behaviour.' Personally, I find it helps to remind myself that this is all part of copying the life of Jesus and, in so doing, discovering my deepest humanity. Service was one of the four main components of Jesus' life,[5] and it is an outworking of the principle that it is in losing our lives for Jesus and the gospel that we shall find them.[6] If we are to copy Jesus in building lives around worship, study, solitude and service, then mission will occupy a significant proportion of our emotional and psychological lives – and result in activity.

It is as we take on mission that Jesus promises us his Spirit. It is as if we can only know that sense of Jesus' life within us, so strongly that we can almost feel him breathing in us, when we are following in his missionary steps. The way to fly like a wild goose is not to stand hopefully on the top of the cliff hoping for a gust of wind to come along; it is to throw ourselves over the edge so that the updrafts can carry us into the sky.

If you are going to be a goose, at least be a wild goose.

Mission as healing the creation

So do we all have to become vicars, nuns or missionaries? I hope some of us will, but, no, of course not. If the Jesus-life is our blueprint for what it is to be fully human, then it would be absurd to limit it to just a few 'professional Christians'. Mark Greene used to work for one of the major advertising agencies. He has compiled an amusing hierarchy of Christian acceptability in the church:

Pastor

Overseas Missionary

Full-time Christian Worker

Tentmaker (as long as it's abroad)

Elder

Deacon

Poor Christian

Christian

Rich Christian

Former Advertising Executives[7]

The list raises a smile, but it is not far off the mark in some of our more subconscious thinking. And we can understand why. If we are sent by Jesus on mission, does that not automatically mean becoming missionaries?

It all depends, of course, on what mission is. In John's Gospel, chapter 20, Jesus says that we are sent by him, just as he was sent by the Father. Our mission is patterned on his, and we continue his mission.

Our default understanding of mission is frequently evangelism or evangelization – the process of telling others about Jesus, his death and resurrection for the forgiveness of our sins. This is plainly at least partly in view of that passage in John 20. And it is very important. But can I suggest that mission in the context of John's Gospel (and indeed the whole Bible) means something much broader, of which evangelization is a part? Jesus understood his mission in terms of the healing and renewal of all the creation.

John begins his Gospel with the famous prologue (chapter 1:1–18). He starts it with the very same words that begin the Bible in the book of Genesis: 'In the beginning'.[8] The following verses show us 'the Word' (Jesus) as the agent of creation, in whom is life itself. The first few verses of John's Gospel bring out multiple correspondences with the opening verses of Genesis.

What is John doing? He is showing us that Jesus was intimately involved in the creation of the cosmos. And he is announcing that this creative Word, through whom the world and everything in it was made, has now actually stepped into his creation. The Word comes as the Creator into his own creation.

Much of the Gospel is structured around signs that Jesus performs.[9] These are pointers to his 'glory'.[10] The first of these signs is the famous turning of water into wine at a wedding in Cana of Galilee.[11] This is not just some splendid magic trick to dazzle the crowds, nor is it a parable that we can have more fun in life with Jesus than without him. The presence of wine at a wedding feast is a calculated demonstration that Jesus is the one who will fulfil all the Old Testament promises to see the whole earth full of the glory of God as the waters cover the sea. Jesus the Word is bringing the work of creation to its fulfilment.

Many of the signs carry strong connotations of creation renewed or healed. Jesus raises a child from his deathbed.[12] He feeds a huge crowd from a few loaves and fish.[13] He walks on water.[14] He opens the eyes of a man born blind, by mixing his saliva with the mud on the ground.[15] He brings Lazarus out from his grave.[16] All are interventions to restore human beings or to exercise dominion over creation, or to reverse the effects of sin and death on the created order.

And John's Gospel reaches its climax with the resurrection. John begins chapter 20 with the words, 'Early on the first day of the week, while it was still dark, Mary Magdalene went to the tomb . . . ' Once more John is evoking the language of

Genesis 1, when on the first day of the creation of the world, 'darkness was over the surface of the deep'.[17] When Jesus appears, gloriously alive, he does so in a garden, with Mary mistaking him for the gardener.[18] John is telling us that Jesus has destroyed the power of death that was defacing and destroying the original creation. Now creation can begin again, free from death. And just as the first Adam was the original gardener in Eden, in the original creation, now Jesus is the second Adam, in whom all the human race can be renewed and recommissioned to steward and govern the new creation.

Jesus was sent to set creation free from death. He was to open the gate to life and healing for the human race and the entire creation. The lynchpin to all this was that sin should be dealt with. It is sin that binds humanity to death. At the cross, Jesus deals with sin once for all ('It is finished'[19]). This is why the basis on which forgiveness can be assured is so central to Jesus' commission to the apostles.[20] It is also why sin and its effects on human flourishing are so regularly and thoughtfully considered throughout John's Gospel.[21]

In the context of John's Gospel then, to be sent by Jesus as the Father sent him is to be sent to restore creation to life in the fullest possible sense. We engage with Jesus through his life-giving Spirit in the great work of resurrecting a dead universe, healing a sick world, bringing forgiveness to a blind humanity.

The image of God restored – for mission

In the next chapter we will think more about what being sent may mean for us in practice. Before moving to the practicalities, notice that this idea of healing the creation is nothing less than the original mandate that God gave to Adam and Eve in the Garden of Eden: 'God blessed them and said to them, "Be fruitful and increase in number; fill the earth and subdue it. Rule over the fish in the sea and the birds in the sky and over every living creature that moves on the ground.'"[22] This commission to steward the creation well and wisely comes immediately after the idea that men and women are made in God's image,[23] with both ideas being expressly linked in the verse before that.[24] Human beings were created by God to have this healing leadership over creation. We have come full circle – this was the key idea of the first chapter.

Now we see this original mandate restored, and cast in terms of mission.[25] To be sent by Jesus is to be commissioned again back into our full humanness. He is calling us back into what we were created to be and do. Our Christian mission answers most deeply the way we are made as human beings.

Working it all out

John's desire to stop being a farm goose and to become a wild goose will involve him in two things: a willingness to be sent by Jesus into the world, and a vision for the whole of life as an arena for mission.

I once heard a brilliant talk by Rowan Williams, the Archbishop of Canterbury. He related the callings of human beings, not least from the Genesis accounts of Adam and Eve, to how Christians today can see ourselves as metaphorical (and some actual) politicians, artists and gardeners. The politicians were called to the construction of society, the artists to the understanding and celebration of all things, and the gardeners to the loving and careful nurturing of all created things. I loved how he helped us to see that each area of human life was part of what we were created (and, in Christ, recreated) to be involved in as Christians.

Jesus spoke about 'the renewal of all things, when the Son of Man sits on his glorious throne',[26] and Paul of how God through 'Jesus was pleased . . . to reconcile to himself all things, whether things on earth or things in heaven, by making peace through his blood, shed on the cross'.[27] Through his cross, Jesus brings reconciliation to an alienated and divided world, and through his great kingship, he will bring about the renewal of all things. If we understand mission in the broad terms of renewal and reconciliation, we have a mandate for living every part of our lives in the way that Jesus lived his. Christian scholar, poet and Bible translator Eugene Peterson interprets 1 Thessalonians 4:7 like this: 'God hasn't invited us into a disorderly, unkempt life but into something holy and beautiful.'[28] If we keep this broad understanding of mission rooted in the cross of Christ, as Paul does, and in the coming fulfilment of everything under the loving rule of Christ, as Jesus himself does, then our mission in the world will always be thoroughly Christian.

I once heard a man talking about the difference that becoming a Christian had made to his life. He said that, for the first time, he noticed the man in the ticket office of the train station where he travelled from each morning on his way to work. He saw him as a human being, probably with a family, living a life with his own hopes and fears, joys and sorrows. He talked to him for the first time, engaged with him, connected with him.

I wear glasses and, at one time in my life, had not been to the opticians for a long time. When I went, I was prescribed new and quite different glasses. When I put them on for the first time, it was an extraordinary experience. I felt as though I was seeing the world differently or even for the first time. I could see clearly – and there really were things I had not been able to see before. But everything was sharper, brighter, better defined and more engrossing.

Somehow, when our humanity is restored in Jesus, we see the world differently. We see it more clearly. And we see it more compassionately. We feel we have a different place in the world, or, rather, that we are rediscovering something fundamental that we have always known at some level, but never quite lived out. Our creativity and our empathy are stirred. We may not be used to thinking of it in these terms, but our whole lives become lives of mission. We are sent by Jesus into the world to make a difference, to heal the creation.

10. What shall I do with my life?

Adam and Lisa are newly married. Lisa grew up within the Christian faith, but Adam has only just become a Christian. She is a project manager with a small firm, and he is a designer. This is an exciting time in their lives. There are so many options open to them, and they are very much enjoying exploring them all.

But in another way, the sheer range of options is bewildering and can even be stressful. Both Adam and Lisa are talented, good at their jobs and have lots of friends. They are committed to their local church and want to be involved, but time is limited. There are also so many options in the life of the church too, all of which seem interesting and important. Sometimes Adam and Lisa feel that the church does not really understand the pressures on their time, and that there is an unrealistic expectation that they could do more than they really feel that they can.

One thing they have done is to join one of the church's mid-week groups. They enjoy this, and good friendships are developing. One day the group leader invites Adam and Lisa out to lunch. When they meet, he asks them how they see their faith being lived out in the world. 'Following Jesus is not just for church,' he says. As soon as he says it, this makes perfect sense to Adam and Lisa, even though they had not thought quite that clearly about it before. They begin to talk about how they might live to please God in every area of their lives.

The conversation moves on to the question of prioritizing their time. They can't do everything they would like to, they just can't. So how could they begin to decide which areas of life and church life they should be involved in? The leader asks them if they would like to join him and his wife one evening for supper, when they could talk more together and pray. They quickly agree.

'The spiritual life is first of all a *life*'

The Christian monk and author Thomas Merton once wrote, 'The spiritual life is first of all a *life*.'[1]

Everything we have been considering points in this direction. Following Jesus is not a religious hobby, but a way of being and living. Some of us respond strongly to the spiritual disciplines, others to the central place of church in following Christ, others to the calling to be right out there in the world to share in God's work of healing the creation. The liberated disciple will embrace all three aspects of following Jesus in some way that matches with their personality. But whatever else it means, it means the involvement of the whole of our lives – 'The spiritual life is first of all a *life*.'

Sharing in the healing of creation

So, what might Adam and Lisa have talked about when, together with their home group leader and his wife, they thought how the whole of their lives could express their faith? Taking their cue from the governing idea of mission as 'the healing of creation', here are seven areas that they could have covered.

1. Caring for the environment
God's ongoing care for his creation, through responsible steward-ship, is something central to Christian discipleship. To our shame, the church has often been led by secular agencies here, but it should really be the other way round.

2. Good work practices
We see that the privilege of work is something that springs centrally from our calling to bear God's image. Often when we become Christians, we can have a tendency to despise the workaday world and see it as something boring in contrast to the new excitements of the Christian life, even something that hinders us from getting on with God's 'real work' – that is, church-based activity. But this is a terrible distortion of God's image in us. Part of our responsible stewardship of creation is to do our jobs well and responsibly. Our work (if we are fortunate enough to be in paid employment) is just as much part of our discipleship as coming to church on a Sunday.

3. Running the home
It may sound old fashioned, but it seems to me that part of the 'image of God' mandate is the good running of our homes and the bringing up of our families. This is part of creation, and we are called on to take our roles in stewarding the creation with seriousness. Nowhere is this more true than in the bringing up of children. Parenting, and creating and running a home, are callings which are held in the highest honour.

4. The arts and sciences
Creation is to be reverenced and respected (but never worshipped). Our own special role in the managing of creation necessitates

good science, always carried on in a spirit of wonder and worship. And the arts too have a special role in understanding and celebrating what it is to be part of God's creation in all of its complexity and glory. Theologian Colin Gunton wrote: 'Wherever there is truth, goodness and beauty; wherever things turn out to be what they were created to be, there is to be experienced the work of the perfecting Spirit, giving access to the created world.'[2]

5. Working for peace and justice

Wherever God's plans to heal creation are thwarted, there the work of God's people is to be found. This has inescapable political dimensions. Working with, and for, the poor, relieving those in debt, working in the justice system, brokering peace and reconciliation where there is conflict – all of these are arenas for discipleship.

6. Rejoicing in the everyday

As we've noted, there is a tendency to see the arena of God's work as being the church, on the one hand, as opposed to the everyday world, on the other. There is also the sense that the work of the Spirit is always dramatic and ecstatic, and our daily lives (not, on the whole, being ecstatic all the time!) therefore have nothing to do with the Holy Spirit. But if the healing of creation is our central role in bearing the image of God, if our full humanity is played out in the everyday, then our workaday worlds are full of the glory of God and daily invitations to walk with him. The kitchen, the underground, the coffee bar, changing nappies, the computer, walking the dog, the old people's home, fixing the car, painting the spare room – all these are just as much holy ground and sacred activities as the church service.

Colin Gunton, again, explains that the Holy Spirit 'teaches us to find perfection in the ordinary and power in weakness. That is the way things are transformed this side of the end.'[3]

7. Evangelization and healing

Jesus is the gateway to the healed creation, its source, guide and goal. 'For us there is but one God, the Father, from whom all things came and for whom we live; and there is but one Lord, Jesus Christ, through whom all things came and through whom we live.'[4] It is through faith in him that we ourselves are restored into the image of God, and liberated to play our part in the healing of creation. Along with worship, the task of proclaiming Jesus as the world's true Lord and Saviour, and the prototype of fully human life, is central to our work here on earth.

When we consider how closely Jesus linked the proclamation of the kingdom of God with the ministry of healing the sick in his own practice,[5] it makes us consider how we may make the link between evangelism and healing more explicit. To link prayer for healing with the proclamation of Jesus as the king of the realm of God is Jesus' own model. Throughout the ages, the church has continually pioneered health care alongside its missionary work. And it is always true to say that, wherever the forgiveness of sins is experienced in the name of Jesus, there comes peace and the first stages of the healing of a life.

It is through the cross of Jesus that the creation is to find its healing, its reconciliation and renewal. In a sense, all of these seven areas can only be fully understood and experienced in the light of Jesus' death and resurrection, and the gift of the Holy Spirit. The church's primary tasks then remain worship and the proclamation of Jesus and his gospel. In our own lives, everything is to be seen in the glorious light of Jesus, the crucified and risen Son of God, and Saviour of the world.

As a whole, if we take seriously God's work of healing creation, then the remit of mission is really everything that makes for human flourishing. Jesus is looking for good and faithful ministers, evangelists and missionaries, but he is also looking for followers who will be good teachers and film-makers, parents and local councillors, physicists and medics, neighbours and cooks, engineers and ornithologists. He wants Christians who see these things as part of their lives lived out of love for God, and in conformity with their call to live the fully human, Jesus-life.

Discovering my role

So, what are Adam and Lisa to do? This all seems so wide-ranging; how can they discover what their part in it all might be?

The most helpful diagnostic tool for understanding ourselves I have come across is S-H-A-P-E.[6] It is especially useful because it takes our creation seriously (and so is bang in line with the theological understanding of discipleship as the fully human life). The acronym stands for the following.

S piritual gifts
God has given to each of us gifts from his Spirit, what church leader Rick Warren calls 'special God-empowered abilities for serving him'.[7] It is a fair assumption that the gifts God has given to us are likely to reflect the areas of life he wants us to serve him in. Do take the New Testament lists as broadly as possible. They are in Romans 12, 1 Corinthians 12, Ephesians 4 and 1 Peter 4, and cover areas from speaking in tongues, prophecy and gifts of healings to administration, serving, giving and leadership. Do remember that the gifts are for others' benefit rather than our own fulfilment.

H eart's desire
This is what we feel to be at the heart and soul of our person-alities. What are we passionate about? What keeps us up talking late into the night? What do we read about, follow and find we can generally talk about for ever? Don't be over-spiritual about this. I read about one man who was a passionate surfer before he became a Christian. After he turned to Christ, it was the most natural thing in the world for him to start a Christian

youth club for young people who wanted to learn how to surf.
Good plan.

A bilities

What are we actually good at? For some of us this is an easy
question to answer, but for others not so easy. Try asking other
people who know us well and will give us honest feedback.
Parents, spouses and good friends can do this well, if we brief
them carefully. Again, do range widely on this one. Are you a
talented musician, good with computers, a numbers or a words
person?

P ersonality

What kind of a person are we? At one level, are we an extrovert
(deriving our energy from other people) or an introvert (needing
time alone to recharge our batteries)? At another, do we thrive
on order or chaos? Are we an 'up front' type of person or more
'backstage' by temperament? God's call to us will not do violence
to our temperaments.

E xperience

Can we discern a track as we look back on our lives and, if so,
where is it leading? Do remember that God can use both good
and bad experiences in our lives. Maybe he can take something
dreadful from your past, and use you and your understanding
of such things to help others in similar situations.

Another fruitful approach[8] is to imagine that you are at your
own funeral. Four people are to give speeches: someone from
your family, a close friend, someone from work and someone
from church. What do you want them to say? This is a way of
thinking more deeply about what we want our lives to be about.
Once we know that, we can take some steps to move in that
general direction.

It is a huge question to consider how God has made us, and
how this might help us discern where he wants us to share with

Jesus in the work of healing the creation. For some of us, this is an angst-ridden journey. Try to relax, trusting the Lord. Don't be in a hurry, and be willing to make mistakes. Others will be much more happy-go-lucky. It would be good to talk with some friends about this. You would not want to miss out on fulfilling your potential in life.

Working it all out

Let's finish with one famous incident in the life of Jesus. He is in the upper room with his disciples. He is about to face betrayal, and the cross is coming next. To the astonishment of the disciples, he takes a bowl of water, removes his outer clothing and washes their feet – the task normally done by a slave. Then this:

> When he had finished washing their feet, he put on his clothes and returned to his place. 'Do you understand what I have done for you?' he asked them. 'You call me "Teacher" and "Lord", and rightly so, for that is what I am. Now that I, your Lord and Teacher, have washed your feet, you also should wash one another's feet. I have set you an example that you should do as I have done for you. Very truly I tell you, servants are not greater than their master, nor are messengers greater than the one who sent them. Now that you know these things, you will be blessed if you do them.'[9]

What a scene, one that they would never forget! In word and deed, Jesus teaches them profoundly what it is to be a disciple. These lessons are a summary of much of what this book has been about.

When Jesus washes the disciples' feet, it must have been humbling for them, and there must have been a kind of shocking intimacy to the action. He touched their feet – that part of them which was, in the culture of the time and place, one of the least presentable parts of the body, and which, after a long day in the

Jerusalem heat, dust and dirt, must have been caked black with grime and sweat.

Jesus' act of washing the disciples is a picture of what he will do on the cross. His blood cleanses us from all sin. Christian discipleship begins, not with goodness, but with forgiveness.

Of course, we do not have an exact blueprint from Jesus for every situation in life. We have alternative ways to care for and serve others than washing hot and dirty feet. At one level, modern life is very different from that of the first century. At another, Jesus' life was his own life and not ours – he never married, was never old.

But his is *the* life. Because of the wonder of who he is and because he shows us the ultimate human life, there is more than enough in his life for us to fund the living of our own lives. It is as if we have the first three movements of the greatest symphony ever written, but it is up to us to improvise the fourth and last movement. We know enough of the themes and mood of the symphony; we know where it is going to end. We now have the thrill of putting together a score and a performance of the entire work.

So there is enough for us to think how Jesus would handle the loss of a job, rebuild a marriage, cope with old age or handle the family budget, depression, or the birth of a child. He is extraordinary, and we shall never come to the end of discovering his wisdom and the sheer richness of his life.

To be a disciple is to live the blessed life

Did you notice how Jesus concluded his remarks to his disciples with a blessing? 'Now that you know these things, you will be blessed if you do them.'

At one level, we are back with the challenge of the wild geese. The blessing is only for those of us who actually do what Jesus has been teaching us to do. The discipled life may be rooted in hidden tracts of solitude and study, and private prayer and study, but it will result in action, in service. And it is in the service that

Jesus promises this special blessing. The Jesus-life is a life of blessing. It is a good life. It is enjoyable, fulfilling, right and true. We will not regret living in this way.

The language of 'blessing' returns us to Genesis and the accounts of the creation of the world. As God makes Adam and Eve in his own image, he also blesses them. 'God blessed them and said to them, "Be fruitful and increase in number; fill the earth and subdue it. Rule over the fish in the sea and the birds in the sky and over every living creature that moves on the ground."'[10] Blessing is God's favour and kindness, which is powerful and makes things happen. The original blessing produced fruitfulness and expansion. It gave rise to Adam and Eve ruling creation. It gave them their place in the world under God. Blessing is the seal on what it means to be a human being in the world.

So when Jesus pronounces a blessing on his followers as they lead the Jesus-life in serving each other and the world, he is once again renewing humanity in its original creation design and mandate. This way to live is *the* human way to live. This is the way to be truly alive, to find joy and fruitfulness in life. It is not a life of religious plodding or constriction, motivated by shame, guilt and fear. It is world transforming through crucifixion and resurrection. It gives us lives that are useful, purposeful, creative and flourishing.

The Jesus way of being human is different from the old Adam way. It is the difference between a plant, pot-bound, unwatered, straining for light and dying from neglect, and a glorious bed of border plants bursting into life in the spring, dazzling in their colours, exuberant in their life and growth. The pot plant is all on its own on a window sill inside an overheated house. The border is outside, where plants truly grow and flourish, and it works best as a border, not as isolated plants. It is the overall picture that is so breath-taking and overwhelming.

Just so with the new humanity that following Jesus brings into existence. It works best with others – it is the church that is the blaze of colour and life. Each plant within the border has its own life and its own contribution to make, but it is in the whole that the complete drama is seen, which can impact the whole garden. And it is for the outside world, not the hermetically-sealed private world of a house.

This is the way of life to which Jesus calls us. It is not a journey of guilt and failure, stuffy religion or a kind of churchy strait-jacket. It is the way of life and peace. It is not just about one part of our lives (the so-called Christian bit) but about every part of us and every part of our lives and of our friendships. It is about dying at the cross with Jesus, rising again with him as a new and different person, and then finding that, in Jesus, we have found our own truest and most authentic selves. And in losing ourselves, we have found Jesus himself. And in finding him, we have come to share in his great work of bringing the world back to life and freedom.

It is the blessed life, the life that is life indeed. It is the fully human life. 'Now that you know these things, you will be blessed if you do them.'

Notes

Preface (pages 13–16)

1. Roman Catholic Archbishop of El Salvadore, assassinated on 24 March 1980 in a small hospital chapel.
2. Mark 8:35.

Chapter 1. Learning to do life (pages 17–27)

1. Colossians 1:13, 15.
2. It is the same train of thought as in the beginning of the letter to the Hebrews: 'The Son is the radiance of God's glory and the exact representation of his being' (Hebrews 1:3). Jesus is the outshining of the glory of God, and the stamp of God's own being. Again, we find it at the beginning of John's Gospel – 'No-one has ever seen God, but the one and only [Son], who is himself God and is in closest relationship with the Father, has made him known' (John 1:18).
3. Genesis 1:26–27.
4. Romans 5:12–21.
5. Philippians 2:8.

6. Romans 5:19.
7. Romans 5:17 (NIV).
8. Romans 5:18.
9. Romans 5:19.
10. Genesis 1:26.
11. Romans 5:17.
12. Romans 5:17.

Chapter 2. Becoming human (pages 29–42)

1. Irenaeus, *Adversus Haereses*, V.i.1, cited in Alister McGrath, *Christian Theology: an Introduction* (Blackwell, 2001), p. 408.
2. This thinking is based on the correlation in Scripture between human beings as part of God's *creation*, and Christians as part of his *new creation*. This shows us that we can expect clear links between what we are by creation and what we are once we have become Christians. God does not simply ignore or negate our pre-Christian personalities and experiences, but rather redeems them – forgiving and renewing them.
3. Mark 12:30 and parallels.
4. Romans 12:1.
5. Romans 6:13.
6. 1 Corinthians 9:27.
7. Romans 12:2.
8. Ephesians 4:17.
9. Romans 1:21.
10. Romans 8:5–7.
11. Philippians 4:8.
12. Proverbs 4:23.
13. Matthew 18:35.
14. Matthew 5:8.
15. Mark 7:21–23.

16. Jeremiah 17:9.
17. Mark 7:6, quoting Isaiah 29:13.
18. From the song 'I need a new heart', by Andy Piercy, from the Album *Praise God from whom all blessings flow*, by Andy Piercy and David Clifton. Lyric used by kind permission of IQ Music Ltd.
19. Ezekiel 36:26–27.
20. Philippians 2:13.
21. John 3:7.
22. Andrei Platanov, *Nursery of the New Man*, quoted in James Meek's *The People's Act of Love* (Canongate, 2005).
23. 2 Corinthians 5:17.
24. Exodus 6:7.
25. Isaiah 11:7.
26. Zechariah 8:4–5.
27. For instance, Matthew 22:1–4.
28. Revelation 21:2 and 22:1–5.
29. 1 Corinthians 15:33, from the Greek poet Menander.
30. 'Christ in you, the hope of glory' (Colossians 1:27).

Chapter 3. Copying Jesus (pages 43–56)

1. Colossians 3:17.
2. 1 Corinthians 11:1.
3. John 13:14–15.
4. Mark 3:14–15.
5. Matthew 4:23.
6. Matthew 10:7–8.
7. Acts 9:36–43.
8. Mark 5:37–43.
9. Luke 11:1–2.
10. Both prophecy and typology are ways of seeing how the Old Testament looks forward to the coming of Jesus, either by way of predicting him in words (prophecy) or

through a person or role who or which finds an ultimate fulfilment in Jesus (typology).

11. Acts 1:1.
12. In this, as in so much, I am following Dallas Willard's analysis in his magnificent book, *The Divine Conspiracy* (HarperCollins, 1997).
13. Luke 4:16.
14. Luke 6:12–13.
15. Mark 6:32, 46.
16. Mark 15:32–42.
17. John 17:1–26.
18. Matthew 11:25.
19. Mark 14:26.
20. John 5:19.
21. Mark 8:35; John 12:25.
22. Luke 2:41–50.
23. Mark 12:35–37; John 10:34–35.
24. Matthew 4:1–11.
25. Mark 15:34, quoting Psalm 22:1.
26. Luke 4:18–19, quoting Isaiah 61:1–2 and 58:6.
27. e.g. Mark 10:45; Ezekiel 2:1; Daniel 7:13.
28. Mark 10:45, and e.g. Isaiah 42:1–9; 49:1–7; 52:13 – 53:12.
29. Mark 1:35.
30. Mark 2:7.
31. Mark 2:13.
32. Mark 4:35–36.
33. Mark 6:31–32.
34. Mark 6:46.
35. Mark 7:24.
36. Mark 9:2.
37. Mark 9:30–31.
38. Mark 11:11.
39. Mark 14:32–33, 35.
40. Mark 16:6–7.
41. Mark 10:45.

42. Luke 22:27.
43. e.g. Mark 1:36–38.
44. Mark 6:30–44.

Chapter 4. Vision for life with God (pages 57–68)

1. Even though Raj's story is fictional, the bird song illustration is real!
2. Psalm 19:10.
3. Matthew 4:4.
4. Deuteronomy 8:3.
5. Genesis 1:3.
6. Psalm 33:6.
7. Hebrews 1:3.
8. John 11:43–44.
9. John 5:25.
10. 1 Thessalonians 2:13.
11. John 5:39.
12. Luke 24:27.
13. James 1:22.
14. Ephesians 4:24.

Chapter 5. Prayer and life (pages 69–82)

1. Luke 11:1.
2. Matthew 6:9.
3. Matthew 6:9–13.
4. Luke 11:1.
5. Mark 1:35.
6. John 6:15.
7. Luke 4:16.
8. Tom Wright is the Bishop of Durham and a considerable scholar.

9. Tom Wright, *Simply Christian* (SPCK, 2006), p. 142.
10. Published by Church House Publishing.
11. Luke 10:21.
12. Luke 11:1–13.
13. e.g. Romans 8:26–27.
14. How else can we explain Jude 20, where we are encouraged to be 'praying in the Holy Spirit'? If we are encouraged to pray in the Spirit, presumably it is possible, but not advisable, to pray *not* in the Spirit.
15. Romans 8:26–27.
16. Gordon Fee sometimes translates the Greek word as 'S/spirit' in his monumental study of Paul's teaching about the Holy Spirit, *God's Empowering Presence* (Hendrickson, 1994).
17. 1 Corinthians 14:16.
18. Matthew 26:38.
19. Luke 22:44.
20. Hebrews 5:7.
21. Romans 8:26.
22. Colossians 1:9–10.
23. W. H. Auden, letter to Louise Bogan, 18 May 1942, quoted in John Haffenden (Ed.), *W. H. Auden: The Critical Heritage* (Routledge, 1997), p. 356.

Chapter 6. When life is hard (pages 83–94)

1. Hazel Rolston expresses this well in her book *Beyond the Edge*: 'Was I some sort of diva who expected to say, "I'm a Christian – get me out of here", and demand a life made up of garish threads?' (Inter-Varsity Press, 2008), p. 155.
2. Mark 8:34.
3. John 12:23–26.

4. Volunteering with the Besom Foundation, a Christian organisation which acts as a bridge between those in need and those who want to help.
5. John 16:33.
6. Matthew 27:46.
7. 'Surely he took up our pain and bore our suffering' (Isaiah 53:4).

Chapter 7. Why go to church? (pages 95–110)

1. Matthew 16:18; 18:17.
2. Lesslie Newbigin, *The Household of God* (SCM, 1953), p. 27.
3. Lesslie Newbigin, *The Gospel in a Pluralist Society* (Eerdmans, 1989), p. 227.
4. Matthew 1:16; cf. 1:17.
5. This comes out in several fascinating ways. For a start, Jesus is named 'because he will save his *people* from their sins' (Matthew 1:21 – italics mine). Scholars help us see how Matthew writes his Gospel as a new Torah (the first five books of the Old Testament, sometimes referred to as 'the law'). Jesus is the new Moses, going up a mountain to bring, not the ten commandments, but the Sermon on the Mount (Matthew 5:1–2). And in calling twelve disciples to him and giving them authority to bring healing and freedom from evil, and sending them out into all the world, he is in effect reconstituting the pattern of the twelve tribes of Israel from the Old Testament (Matthew 10:1–4).
6. Matthew 22:1–14.
7. Geoffrey Wainwright, *Doxology: The Praise of God in Worship, Doctrine, and Life*, 2, 3, quoted in James Emery White (Inter-Varsity Press, 2004), p. 142.
8. Richard J. Foster, *The Celebration of Discipline*, 148, quoted in James Emery White (Inter-Varsity Press, 2004), p. 142.

9. Matthew 28:19–20.
10. Matthew 4:19.
11. Matthew 10.

Chapter 8. Learning to love (pages 111–121)

1. Colossians 3:11.
2. N. T. Wright, *Colossians and Philemon* (Inter-Varsity Press, 1986), pp. 140–141.
3. e.g. Matthew 18:15.
4. Matthew 12:49–50.
5. Luke 15:2.
6. Luke 7:39.
7. Matthew 11:19.
8. Matthew 18:5, 6.
9. Matthew 18:12–14.
10. David Clark, *Yes to Life*, quoted in *Community and Growth* by Jean Varnier (Darton Longman and Todd, second revised edition 1989), p. 4.
11. e.g. Matthew 18:15–20; Matthew 5:23–26; Matthew 5:21–22.
12. It is also worth bearing in mind Paul's wise words from Romans 12:18: 'If it is possible, as far as it depends on you, live at peace with everyone.' While the ideal is to be at peace with all, it may not be possible. Some people just will not respond to overtures of peace, and you can only do so much.
13. C. S. Lewis, *The Screwtape Letters* (Geoffrey Bles, 1942), pp. 15–17.
14. In the book originally of the same name, now John Stott, *The Message of Ephesians: God's New Society* (Inter-Varsity Press, 1979).

Chapter 9. Healing the creation (pages 123–132)

1. Paraphrased by Steve Chalke and Anthony Watkins in *Intelligent Church* (Zondervan, 2006), p. 26.
2. John 20:21–23.
3. I think the best way of understanding the way in which the apostles are given the power, both to forgive sins and to withhold forgiveness, is to see that Jesus is entrusting them with the message of the gospel: if anyone responds to Jesus' death on the cross with repentance and faith, then the apostles can proclaim that they are forgiven. On the other hand, if their message is refused, they need to say that their hearers are not forgiven. The cross is God's appointed way to the forgiveness of sins, and so to reject the cross is to reject God's offer of forgiveness.
4. From 'Citizenship in a Republic', delivered at the Sorbonne in Paris on 23 April, 1910, quoted in Steve Chalke and Anthony Watkins, *Intelligent Church*, p. 28.
5. See chapter 3.
6. Mark 8:35.
7. Mark Greene, *Thank God It's Monday* (Scripture Union, 1994), pp. 16–17.
8. John 1:1; Genesis 1:1.
9. John 20:30–31.
10. John 2:11.
11. John 2:1–11.
12. John 4:46–54.
13. John 6:1–12.
14. John 6:16–21.
15. John 9:6–7.
16. John 11:38–44.
17. Genesis 1:2.
18. John 20:15.
19. John 19:30, cf. 19:28.
20. John 20:23.

21. e.g. John 1:29; 5:14, cf. 9. 3; 8:23–24; 9:39–41; 16:8–11.
22. Genesis 1:28.
23. Genesis 1:27.
24. Genesis 1:26.
25. Other places in the New Testament bring this out too. Colossians 1:15–20 is a magnificent hymn, showing Jesus to be the supreme Lord of both the original and the new creations by using 'image of God' language. Paul moves on to show how the church, in proclaiming the gospel, is bringing reconciliation to 'every creature under heaven' (21–23). Similarly, in Romans 8:18–30, he shows how the whole of creation is being healed through the restoration of humanity back to its original image of God. Tom Wright puts it well: 'The creation . . . is waiting – on tip toe with expectation, in fact – for the particular freedom it will enjoy when God gives to his children that glory, that wise rule and stewardship, which was always intended for those who bear God's glorious image' (*Paul for Everyone. Romans Pt 1* [SPCK, 2004], p. 152).
26. Matthew 19:28.
27. Colossians 1:19–20.
28. In *The Message* translation of the Bible.

Chapter 10. What shall I do with my life? (pages 133–143)

1. Thomas Merton, *Thoughts in Solitude*, 46, quoted in White (Inter-Varsity Press, 2004), p. 75.
2. Colin Gunton, *The Christian Faith* (Blackwell, 2002), p. 178.
3. ibid., p. 172.
4. 1 Corinthians 8:6.
5. e.g. Matthew 4:23; 9:35; 10:7–8.
6. Written up in Rick Warren, *The Purpose Driven Life* (Zondervan, 2002) chapters 30–32, although I have heard it talked about elsewhere too from the mid-1990s. See also

the useful summary and discussion in James Lawrence, *Growing Leaders* (CPAS 2004), pp. 103–106.

7. Rick Warren, *The Purpose Driven Life*, p. 236.
8. From Stephen R. Covey, *The Seven Habits of Highly Effective People* (Simon & Schuster, 1989).
9. John 13:12–17.
10. Genesis 1:28.